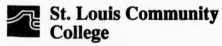

Paranoia, the Bomb, and 1950s Science Fiction Films

Paranoia, the Bomb, and 1950s Science Fiction Films

Cyndy Hendershot

Bowling Green State University Popular Press
Bowling Green, OH 43403

Copyright 1999 © Bowling Green State University Popular Press

Library of Congress Cataloging-in-Publication Data
Hendershot, Cynthia.
    Paranoia, the bomb, and 1950s science fiction films / Cyndy
Hendershot.
       p.   cm.
    Includes bibliographical references.
    ISBN 0-87972-799-3 (hardcover). -- ISBN 0-87972-800-0 (pbk.)
    1. Science fiction films--United States--History and criticism.
I. Title.
PN1995.9.S26H37 1999
791.43'615--dc21
                                       999-26483
                                            CIP

Cover design by Dumm Art

For Antony with love

CONTENTS

ACKNOWLEDGEMENTS

A big thanks to Antony Oldknow of Eastern New Mexico University to whom this book is dedicated for his continual support and reading of drafts. Thanks as always to Miss D.

I want to thank Bruce Clarke of Texas Tech University for his helpful suggestions regarding this project. I want to thank the staff of The National Atomic Museum in Albuquerque, New Mexico, for allowing me to use their archives.

My gratitude to Arkansas State University for a summer research grant that helped this project. My appreciations as well to the two readers at Bowling Green State University Popular Press, Donald Palumbo and Gary Hoppenstand whose insightful comments were very helpful.

A version of Chapter 1 appeared in *American Imago* 54.1. A version of Chapter 2 appeared in the *Journal of American Culture* 20.1. A version of Chapter 3 appeared in *Extrapolation* 39.1. A version of Chapter 4 appeared in *Readerly/Writerly Texts* 4.2, copyright 1997. A version of Chapter 5 appeared in *Science-Fiction Studies* 25. A version of Chapter 6 appeared in *Literature and Psychology* 45. A version of Chapter 7 appeared in *Mosaic* 33. All reprinted with permission.

INTRODUCTION

Giant ants, prehistoric monsters brought back to life, humans replaced by uncanny doubles—these and other elements characterize the 1950s B-science fiction film. While the cult-following films such as *Them!, The Beast from 20,000 Fathoms,* and *Invasion of the Body Snatchers* have often predicated on ironic laughter at films frequently considered to be no more than museum pieces, this study takes a very different approach to such films and others related to them. In my contrastive view, 1950s sf films open a window on the cultural paranoia that characterized America at this time, a cultural paranoia largely triggered by the discovery and use of nuclear weapons during World War II.[1]

I read these films both within a psychoanalytic conception of paranoia and within the historical context of what constituted cultural paranoia for postwar America. I believe that paranoia provides a strong model for analysis of sf film, especially because film makes possible a visual forum for representing the totalizing systems of the paranoiac.[2] The worlds created by sf films provide a representation of the visual, frequently cinematic delusions of paranoiacs. Film supplies a medium whereby the auditory and visual hallucinations of paranoia can approach a tangible existence on the screen. Thus what might be called metaphorically the private film in the head of the individual paranoiac may be transformed into a systematized light-and-sound delusion available to an audience.

In a time when we are re-evaluating the cultural paranoia that shaped Cold War American life, re-examination of how popular entertainment both reflected and shaped this paranoia provides a means of helping us to come to terms with a recent past in which paranoiac logic resulted in human radiation experiments, executions, and blacklisting— to name just a few postwar ills.

Although I use clinical case studies of paranoia as touchstones for understanding paranoiac systems, my concern here is with a cultural paranoia in which delusion moved beyond individual psychosis into what was almost universally accepted in the postwar period as social reality.

It is my argument that the sf films I have chosen to examine represent different metaphorical embodiments of a varied and complex cultural paranoia. Postwar paranoia may have stemmed from the atomic bomb, but it came to correlate with a much wider range of public items and events, being clearly linked also to such subjects as anti-communism, internal totalitarianism, scientific progress, domestic problems, gender roles, and sexuality. Indeed paranoia was, at the very least, a background coloring for the whole life of the period, public and private. *Invasion of the Body Snatcher*'s Miles Bennel's *cri-de-coeur*—"You're next!"—is a telling image of paranoiac panic.[3] Though pervasive, the quality of postwar paranoia was, in fact, cloudy and unfocused, and its very nebulousness allowed it multi-faceted metaphorical expression. There was a widespread feeling that "You're next for something"; however, that something kept constantly changing—alien invasion, communist takeover, nuclear war, dehumanization, or some other horror. Yet the very ubiquitousness of the phenomenon in all its facets is what gave postwar paranoia its gripping power over American society, whether in politics, film, or in everyday life.

Why B-sf films? On the one hand, I believe, along with many other critics, that the status of sf as a degraded genre allowed these films a freedom not possessed by the more serious realistic dramas of the time.[4] Further, the non-realistic qualities of sf film also provided a forum in which fear of nuclear war and other fears could be explored on a metaphorical level, a level which appealed to and revealed postwar fantasy about nuclear holocaust. This argument follows Jacques Derrida's famous discussion of nuclear war in which he maintains that the nuclear age is built "by fable, on the basis of an event that has never happened (except in fantasy, and that is not nothing at all)" (23). Derrida goes on to cite Freud's 1897 comment "that there was no difference in the unconscious between reality and a fiction loaded with affect" (23).

The non-realistic framework of science fiction allowed it to create a fantasy space for the cultural paranoia of the Atomic Age. Representing nuclear war in a realistic fashion is, in the final analysis, not artistically successful in my opinion because postwar perceptions of nuclear war exist only in fantasy. Although atomic bombs were used on Hiroshima and Nagasaki, they were not part of a nuclear war, and, further, the American public was sheltered from the reality of the aftermath in those cities. As I discuss later in the study, ruined buildings served as the visual sign for atomic destruction; however, bodies were eerily absent from such representations.

Another reason I have chosen sf films is developed in Chapter One, but deserves brief mention here. The systematized delusory worlds of paranoiacs very frequently resemble worlds created in sf works. One text that serves in this study as a framework for understanding paranoia is Daniel Paul Schreber's *Memoirs of My Nervous Illness* (1903). Schreber's baroque text, which has served as the basis for much psychoanalytic discussion of paranoia due to Freud's classic essay on Schreber, reveals a world uncannily like fictional sf worlds.

One reason perhaps for the increasing popularity of science fiction in the twentieth century may be related to the comfort of perfectly structured universes which sf offers. Similarly, in troubled times, paranoia offers, whether individually or culturally, the relief afforded by control and meaning within a frightening world. Thus while other genres also represent obliquely many of the Atomic Age concerns explored in this study—*film noir* comes to mind most immediately—I have chosen science fiction because it, like the modern phenomenon of paranoia, is inextricably tied up with science and technology.[5]

The first three chapters of this book focus on science fiction and paranoia, and their relationship to postwar science and technology and representations of them. Chapter One sets up a theoretical basis for interconnections between science fiction as a genre and paranoia as a psychosis and cultural phenomenon that is crucial to the study as a whole. Focusing on both Schreber and Kirk Allen, the pseudonymous name for a Los Alamos scientist who lived in a delusory sf world, this chapter explores how paranoia is tied up with both the increasing scientism that developed in the twentieth century and the trauma that has developed over negative implications of science and technology, especially nuclear weapons.

Chapter Two focuses on accounts of the Manhattan Project and three sf films (*The Day the Earth Stood Still, This Island Earth,* and *Killers from Space*) in order to explore both the paranoiac logic employed by the scientists' movement and the representations of the atomic scientist that were generated in popular 1950s films. Sf films promoted the self-fashioned image of the atomic scientist as a postwar messiah, frequently endorsing while simultaneously questioning notions of scientific progress that fueled the Manhattan Project itself and public perceptions of the atomic scientists following their rise to fame after Hiroshima and Nagasaki.

Chapter Three looks at what many people both then and now have seen as the dark side of nuclear weapons—radiation. I examine how fears of radiation contamination created by non-fiction works such as David Bradley's *No Place to Hide* as well as fictional works such as *Invaders from Mars, It Came from Outer Space,* and *Invasion of the Body Snatchers* centered on delusions of a contaminated body, delusions that are also typical of paranoiac fears. Indeed, the real threat of radiation and a fictional sense of it as supernatural force blur in what is clearly a paranoiac vision.

The second part of the book focuses on postwar paranoia, sf films, and the personal realm, with specific reference to gender. Chapter Four examines what I label feminine paranoia in both accounts written by Los Alamos wives and two sf films (*I Married a Monster from Outer Space* and *Attack of the 50 Ft. Woman*). This chapter explores how the security state with its exclusion of women from knowledge promoted a feminine paranoia that disrupted the domestic realm. The secrecy involved, which had been designed ostensibly to protect women and the home from harm, ironically produced a paranoiac structure which threatened the very foundations of that home.

Chapter Five continues the exploration of gender, science fiction, and paranoia, looking at how these issues were frequently framed within an evolutionary/devolutionary context. Darwinian metaphors pervaded discussions of the Bomb and its impact on postwar society. Similarly, *The Beast from 20,000 Fathoms, Them!* and *The Incredible Shrinking Man* also examine the implications of nuclear weapons from a Darwinian perspective. Further, the latter two films look at both the gendering of nuclear weapons and the impact of this gendering on 1950s masculinity.

Chapter Six examines the sexualization of nuclear weapons and war in postwar popular culture, focusing on two films—*The Creature from the Black Lagoon* and *Revenge of the Creature*—which create a complex metaphor for The Bomb as sexual force and look at the implications of this metaphorical creation for gender roles of the 1950s.

The last section of the book explores two ends of a postwar spectrum, both of which worked to elide the trauma of the bomb. Chapter Seven looks at sf's participation in the postwar mythologizing of the bomb. The films I analyze in this chapter—*Earth Vs. the Flying Saucers, 20 Million Miles to Earth,* and *The Monolith Monsters*—use Greco-Roman and Christian myth to remove nuclear weapons from historical time and thus absolve humans of their responsibility for the destructive power of the weapons.

Chapter Eight examines another postwar strategy for binding the affect of the bomb: portraying it as merely another conventional weapon.[6] Thus, the sf films *Invasion USA* and *The War of the Worlds* represent atomic bombs, but only as bigger kinds of conventional weapons. In my view, such representation has the effect of diminishing a perception of the newness of nuclear weapons and, instead, places them in a familiar context, that of World-War-II combat.

Science fiction films of the 1950s provide an interesting means of understanding how nuclear weapons and nuclear war were metaphorically understood by postwar culture. Within their paranoiac worlds, these films reveal that the only way the Atomic Age makes sense is through a skewed perception of the world. Only within paranoiac logic can radiation contamination, nuclear war, and other postwar horrors make sense.

1

PARANOIA AND THE DELUSION OF THE TOTAL SYSTEM

Post-World-War-II American society is popularly and frequently defined by the symptom of paranoia. The paranoia that pervades the McCarthyist witch-hunts, the "duck-and-cover" policy of civil defense, and postwar representations of the alien invader characterizes late twentieth-century perceptions of 1950s America. Science fiction is the genre most commonly invoked now to represent paranoia of the 1950s, and within that culture it stood as a genre conducive to expressions of fear and paranoia. Los Alamos and the development of the atomic bomb gave rise to numerous cultural texts that attempted to represent what was frequently perceived as the unrepresentable—atomic power. The prehistoric monsters, giant ants, pod people, and other horrors that people 1950s science fiction films attest to what had already been a strong interpenetration between physics and science fiction. The fact that science fiction and paranoiac discourse have affinities becomes manifest in popular science fiction of that period. Yet the links between the totalizing, systematic worlds of science fiction and the delusional systems constructed by the paranoiac have more subtle connections. Sf authors construct comprehensive worlds much as Daniel Paul Schreber creates a complete delusional world in his *Memoirs of My Nervous Illness* (1903).[1] Yet our very conception of paranoia emerges from a discourse located on the boundary between science and fiction—psychoanalysis. In fact Schreber's most famous interpreter, Sigmund Freud, notes the uncomfortable similarities between Schreber's theory and his own.[2] In this chapter I focus on a postwar American text in which issues of science (represented by the atomic physicist), science fiction, paranoia, and psychoanalysis converge: Robert Lindner's fictionalized account of his analytic sessions with a Los Alamos physicist, "The Jet-Propelled Couch," contained in his collection of "true psychoanalytic tales," *The Fifty Minute Hour* (1954).[3] Lindner's tale coincides with postwar science fiction per se through its analysis of paranoia as a symptom of the atomic-bomb project and ultimately through its replication of the very disease it seeks to diagnose. I argue that paranoia may be read as a symptom of a culture in which the totalizing scientific systems characteristic of Newtonian physics continue to haunt an increasingly multiplicitous and non-totalizing view of the world that is emerging in the twentieth century.

In *Order Out of Chaos,* Ilya Prigogine and Isabelle Stengers argue that classical Newtonian physics rests on a world view in which the scientist is conceived as "the potential holder of a universal key to all physical phenomena, thus endowed with a potentially omnipotent knowledge" (21). Classical science hence relies on a view that one totalizing system can explain the universe. Prigogine and Stengers trace developments in nineteenth- and twentieth-century science that point to the limits of classical science. The emergent world view as they see it allows for the replacement of the monolithic reality of the Newtonian system with *realities:* "as randomness, complexity, and irreversibility enter into physics as objects of positive knowledge, we are moving away from this rather nàive assumption of a direct connection between our description of the world and the world itself" (54-55). What I want to propose is that paranoia is a psychosis intertwined with the Newtonian world view and one that ultimately points to the limits of the totalizing classical system as the dream of the classical scientist emerges as delusion.

Lindner's tale focuses on a research physicist in his 30s working at Los Alamos—named "X reservation" in the text—in the 1950s. Kirk Allen, the pseudonymous name of the physicist in Lindner's account, is drafted into working at Los Alamos upon completion of his doctorate. At the end of the war he is discharged, studies abroad for a year, then returns to work at Los Alamos. Allen is referred to Lindner, who is practicing psychoanalysis in Baltimore, by a Los Alamos military official who tells Lindner over the telephone that Allen is normal and hardworking, but believes he lives part of his life on another planet (156). In the course of his analytic sessions with Allen, Lindner discovers that the physicist has constructed a delusional universe to which he periodically travels but in which he has recently been spending more and more time. Allen has compiled twelve-thousand pages of typescript describing his adventures, research, and experiences in a universe in which he is "Kirk Allen, Lord of a planet in an interplanetary empire in a distant universe" (176). In addition to the manuscript, Allen writes a glossary of names and terms, 82 maps drawn to scale, 161 architectural sketches and elevations,12 genealogical tables, a description of the galactic system, a 200-page history of the empire over which Allen serves as Lord, and 306 drawings of the planet (179-80). In the course of the analysis, Lindner adopts a belief in Allen's delusory world in order to, as he theorizes it, dislodge Allen from the psychosis from within (195). Lindner succeeds in eliminating Allen's belief in the delusory universe, but Lindner himself comes to believe in it, leading Lindner to conclude that "I know my chair and the couch are separated only by a thin line" (207).

Allen's system corresponds to the paranoiac's totalizing system and bears many striking similarities to Schreber's delusional theology. One phenomenon that characterizes paranoia is the creation of a totalizing system. Micheline Enriquez notes that "we cannot stress enough the importance for the paranoiac of this *system,* a system which always refers him to an order, to a higher instance" (126). The systemization and theorizing that characterize the paranoiac have led many commentators to associate paranoia with knowledge and knowledge-producing systems *per se.*[4] For Lacan, the formation of the ego is a paranoiac process: hence, taking one's place in the Symbolic Order means living in a paranoiac system that is culturally sanctioned.[5] For my purposes I want to focus on how both Schreber's and Kirk Allen's delusional systems invoke a convergence of theology and science that forms part of their historical worlds. In his preface to the *Memoirs,* Schreber makes just such a connection: "I believe that expert examination of my body and observation of my personal fate during my lifetime would be of value for both science and the knowledge of religious truths" (31). Thus Schreber tells us that he has sacrificed his privacy in order to further knowledge. Schreber addresses his former doctor Flechsig, asking him to verify his delusional experiences because this verification will result in his thesis being regarded as a respectable scientific issue (35).[6] Later Schreber comments that his manuscript is reaching the length of a scientific study, and again emphasizes his purpose to provide empirical evidence for his delusional system (123n). He pleads for medical examination of his body, which he believes will verify that he is being transformed into a woman: this affirmation will serve as clinching evidence that his theology is correct. Schreber is convinced that x-raying his body will demonstrate the change in his skeletal structure from male to female and also prove to the doctors that the destruction wrought on his internal organs by the rays which have been penetrating him is real (248). Schreber closes his *Memoirs* by stating, "I can do no more than *offer my person as object of scientific observation for the judgment of experts. My main motive in publishing this book* is to invite this" (251).

Schreber's conjoining of empirical scientific data and theological theory is typical of *fin-de-siécle* European intellectuals. Schreber wished to use science to verify the existence of God. He used physiological data concerning human nerves to construct a cosmological view of the universe based on the human body. Further, he attempted to situate his narrative within the late nineteenth-century theories of evolution and entropy. Discussing his theory of creation, Schreber comments that he believes in an evolutionary chain, but one in which each link has been created by divine intervention (192). Schreber attempted to resolve the conflict between Darwinian theory and Christian belief, a conflict that he believed victimized him because his studies of the natural sciences had made him doubt Christian literalism (80). So he turned to a typical Victorian "solution" to the dilemma. Schreber, like many Victorians, as Alvar Ellegard points out, adopted the view of absolute creation which argues that "each species arose as a distinct and instantaneous creation" (30). Further Schreber's apocalyptic vision of the destruction of the earth from which he is the sole survivor partakes of entropic images prevalent in the late nineteenth century. Schreber comments that on the day of the destruction of the earth "there was talk of 'clocks of the world' running out and at the same time a continuous rich stream of rays toward my body" (93-94). The moving upward of human life seen as characteristic of Darwinian theory and the apocalyptic dying of the sun which characterized Lord Kelvin's Second Law of Thermodynamics are negotiated in Schreber's delusional system. The crux is that Kelvin's attempt to preserve theology within a scientific theory that Prigogine and Stengers describe as involving "a dizzy leap from engine technology to cosmology" (116) made him an influential and renowned scientist, whereas Schreber's system, which extends human physiology to the cosmological level in order to preserve a divine creator, kept him incarcerated in an asylum.

Schreber's need and ability to create a self-contained system points to cultural ideals that plagued late nineteenth-century European society and 1950s America alike. Why does Schreber's delusional system frame itself within the discourses of science and theology? Why does paranoia become a vital area of study in the late nineteenth and early twentieth centuries? My tentative suggestion is that paranoia has an observable connection with the increasing prevalence of scientific discourse throughout all social discourse and with the sense of inferiority experienced by non-scientists saturated with scientific terminology. As Prigogine and Stengers relate, the early nineteenth century represents the beginning of the popularization of science. As scientific discourse seeped into everyday language, other disciplinary discourses, and popular culture science became "a matter of professional consensus and magistral authority" (67). In order for his delusional system to be valid, Schreber had to frame it within the context of empirical science. He offered his transformed body as proof that his theory was valid, even suggesting that his body be dissected after his death to verify his suppositions (251). Schreber's elaborate system, which he believed to be scientifically provable, was partly predicated on a sense of inferiority in the face of scientific professions which he, as a man of law, could not compete with in a public world in which science was increasingly valorized and glamorized. One goal of the conspiracy that he perceives existing between Flechsig and the elements of the anterior realms of God is to deny the Schreber race "choice of those professions which would lead to closer relations with God, such as that of nerve specialist" (57-58).[7] Schreber's ability to understand the workings of the whole universe granted him a Newtonian scientific power that was denied in his role as *Senatspräsident.*

The anxiety and helplessness experienced by those in non-scientific professions in the late nineteenth and early twentieth centuries is expressed by Henry Adams in his "A Letter to American Teachers of History" (1910), in which he bitterly recounts the pressure on the history profession to conform to current scientific theories, commenting that "the violent contradiction between Kelvin's Degradation and Darwin's Elevation was so profound—so flagrant—so vital to mankind, that the historian of human society must be supposed to have watched with ago- nized interest the direction which science should take; since the decision of palaeontologists would fatally decide his own" (162-63). Adams lamented the inferiority and helplessness the humanities must assume in relation to scientific theory. He feared that the meeting of the humanities and science prevalent in early-twentieth-century society was "converting metaphysics into a branch of physics" (196). Adams viewed the scien- tism that dominated his historical period as benefiting scientific dis- course alone.[8]

Paranoia as a response to the increase in scientific popularization and the prevalence of technological development is a suggestive idea. In addition to the creation of a theoretical system, paranoia is characterized by a preservation of intellectual acumen in the paranoiac. J. Laplanche and J. B. Pontalis defined paranoia as "chronic psychosis characterised by more or less systematised delusion, with a predominance of ideas of ref- erence but with no weakening of the intellect, and, generally speaking, no tendency towards deterioration" (296). William G. Niederland noted apropos of Schreber that paranoia "requires superior intelligence" (31). Freud agreed with Schreber's pronouncement of himself as "a man of superior mental gifts and endowed with an unusual keenness alike of intellect and of observation" (84), and Schreber himself offers "the inde- structibility of my reason" as proof for the validity of his theoretical system (123n). The intellectual ability of Schreber troubled Freud; the intellectual capabilities of Kirk Allen troubled Robert Lindner; the figure of the paranoiac haunts psychoanalysis with his or her ability to con- struct theoretical systems in a manner similar to the scientist and similar to that employed by the intellectual in general.[9]

Paranoiacs themselves, however, are haunted by scientific and technological discourse. In addition to Schreber's scientism, which makes neurology a cosmological theory, other examples appeared in early-twentieth-century discourse. In "A Case of Paranoia Running Counter to the Psychoanalytic Theory of the Disease" (1915), Freud discusses a female paranoiac who believed her lover had hired someone to photograph their lovemaking sessions. As she left her lover's apartment, she saw two men on the stairs whispering, one "carrying something which was wrapped up and looked like a small box," an object the woman took to be a camera (264). While Freud was concerned with discussing the case within his theory of paranoia as the product of repressed homosexuality, I am concerned with the technological basis of the woman's paranoia. The woman constructed a theory in which the photographer hid in the room and photographed her while she was in "a particularly compromising position" (264-65). Anxiety concerning technological development seems to have been a factor in this case.

Similarly, in Victor Tausk's "On the Origin of the 'Influencing Machine' in Schizophrenia" (1919) what characterizes his paranoiacs' delusional systems is the presence of a mysterious machine.[10] Using technical language, Tausk's patients made vague descriptions of machines that controlled them physically and mentally, using technical language, a phenomenon that Tausk attributed to "the progressive popularization of the sciences," but the patients' "knowledge of physics was inadequate to explain" the machine (521). The machine could not be fully understood through the framework of known science: "all of the discoveries of mankind, however, were regarded as inadequate to explain the marvelous powers of this machine" (521). Thus the patient possessed the ability to divine the machine's existence, an ability that elevated the patient above the scientist. Although Tausk concluded that the machines were projections of the patients' genitalia, he also concluded that "the machines produced by man's ingenuity and created in the image of man [were] unconscious projections of man's bodily structure. Man's ingenuity seem[ed] to be unable to free itself from its relation to the unconscious" (556n). Tausk outlined a situation similar to Schreber's: why were Tausk's patients paranoiacs if their projections of the surface of the body were identical to the processes inventors undergo to create machines? The answer was the same as in the case of Schreber: they were not professional scientists, yet they were aware enough of scientific discourse to emulate it in their delusions. What were they creating if not valid scientific theory? They were creating science fiction they lived in on a daily basis.

Schreber's delusional system partakes heavily of the language of science fiction. His belief in "fleeting-improvised men" peopling the world after its destruction and his survival of the destruction can be related to science-fiction discourse prevalent in the late nineteenth century and throughout the twentieth century. Schreber's "miraculously created puppets" (42-43n) relate to the nineteenth-century popularity of the golem, which has become transformed into the robot as a result of the popularity of Karel Capek's *R.U.R.* (1920) and which has become further transformed into the replicant in 1950s science-fiction works such as Don Siegel's *Invasion of the Body Snatchers* (1955) and Robert Heinlein's *The Puppet Masters* (1951). Beliefs like Schreber's in the human who is not really human and ones like his intense belief in his continuing human essence in the face of human replicants, typical of the paranoiac, have become science-fiction staples. Further, Tausk discusses a female patient who believed that a replicant of her body was influencing her and believed further that "her mother, likewise the patient's male and female friends, [were] also under the influence of this machine or similar machines" (529). Similarly, the fascinating figure of the replicant, which characterizes contemporary science-fiction works such as Ridley Scott's *Blade Runner* (1982) and *Star Trek: The Next Generation,* is a common feature of the delusional worlds of paranoiacs.

Schreber's cosmological system further bears resemblances to science fiction discourse through its theorizing that in the universe there are inhabited planets other than earth. God, Schreber theorized, through the light "emanating from the sun and other stars" can "perceive" everything occurring on earth and, Schreber added, "possibly on other inhabited planets" (47). Schreber hinted that the transmigration of souls after human death that occurs through God entering the corpse and absorbing the nerves, which, in Schreber's view, make up the soul, may be one technique God uses to populate other planets (51). Schreber argued that humans may have vague recollections of their earlier existences on other planets. He cited one of the fleeting-improvised men as having led another life as an insurance agent on a distant planet (51). Within the framework of this theory, Schreber explored a concept dear to science fiction, parallel worlds.[11] Discussing a name given to him by one of the voices he heard, he commented that this man was said to be from Poland, but added that he might be from a Poland that exists on another planet (74n).[12] Further, Schreber used the comparison of earth to other planets as a way to minimize "the moral decay" (73n) of earth, arguing that "the inhabitants of earth [are] in comparison distinguished by greater moral purity" (73n). The use of parallel worlds to define the earth as less corrupt is a technique common to science fiction as H. G. Wells's

The War of the Worlds (1898), Ray Bradbury's *The Martian Chronicles* (1946-58), *Invaders from Mars* (1953), and others attest.

For my purposes I want to focus on one more specific aspect of Schreber's *Memoirs* that connects the work to science-fiction discourse and to the increasing science-fact/science-fiction mythology that lies behind the atomic-bomb project. Schreber's emphasis on rays as power-ful, divine forces and as destructive, evil forces characterizes his theory. God as nerve, in Schreber's system, transforms himself into rays in order to make "all things of the created world" (46). The rays have not only incredible creative potential, but also curative value. Schreber com-mented that God can remove human illness through the power of rays (48n). While the rays have curative and creative capabilities, they are also potentially destructive. Thus Schreber believed that "permanent contact with rays" was unmanning him (72). Although he eventually saw a positive goal in this transformation, since through it he would become the mother of a new race of humans, his first perception was that the unmanning was being enacted to transform him into a whore. Schreber also thought that the hostile rays were destroying his internal organs and he perceived a battle occurring within him between "pure" rays and "impure" rays (132). Tausk's paranoiac patients were also obsessed with rays. Tausk discussed the fact that the "influencing machines" discussed by his patients used "rays or mysterious forces" to remove and produce "thoughts and feelings" (521). Tausk detailed how the machine was per-ceived by many male patients as producing seminal emissions which "deprive the patient of his male potency and weaken him" (521). Thus Tausk's patients' rays, like Schreber's, threatened to unman the para-noiac.

For people familiar with postwar reaction to gamma rays and the mythologizing of them as both curative and destructive and as possess-ing the potential to deplete male potency, these associations are sugges-tive.[13] What Schreber and Tausk's patients were suggesting was an increasing interpenetration between physics and science fiction in twen-tieth-century discourse, an interpenetration that found one expression in the popular conception of rays. Spencer R. Weart's study of mythology, physics, and science fiction prior to and during the Atomic Age discusses ways in which x-rays served in the late nineteenth and early twentieth centuries as a site where mythologized views of science were expressed. Weart relates that after Roentgen's discovery of x-rays in 1895—a dis-covery to which Schreber directly alludes (248)—"some people wrote to him [Roentgen] to express fear of his 'death's rays'" (46). Similarly, William L. Laurence, official press commentator for the Manhattan Pro-ject, related that many civilians living in the Los Alamos area believed the secret project was "engaged in the manufacture of a 'death ray'" (129). One central fear was the fear of male sterility due to excessive x-raying: this fear re-emerges as the central anxiety expressed by postwar men *vis-à-vis* radiation, which they fear will damage their sexual drive and reproductive capability.[14] Likewise, as Weart relates, x-rays were perceived as a cure-all to medical problems. Weart relates that in early twentieth-century American and European society "doctors experimented by poking x-ray projectors and radioactive substances into every part of their patients' bodies" (48). Thus, it seems clear that Schreber and Tausk's patients were living both the reality of scientific discovery and the fiction that inextricably was wedded to these discoveries in the popular mind. For the non-scientist, paranoiac discourse may serve as a means of validating existence.

What happens when the scientist is himself paranoiac? Kirk Allen's delusional system exists in the context of one of the most mythologized areas of modern physics—the atomic bomb project. Whereas Schreber's perceived messianic purpose was a personal delusion, Kirk Allen's real life as a member of the Manhattan Project was steeped in messianic discourse. In the prewar and postwar periods, atomic physicists were popularly viewed as mystics and gods. Thus, in his account of his involvement in the Manhattan Project, physicist Richard P. Feynman discusses his explanation of the project to the Oak Ridge Plant, commenting "I was a god coming down from the sky! Here were all of these phenomena that were not understood and never heard of before—but I knew all about it; I could give them facts and numbers and everything else" (122). President Truman's speech announcing the use of the atomic bomb on Hiroshima emphasized that the atomic physicists were a "chosen people" given the knowledge of atomic physics by God: "We thank God that it has come to us, instead of to our enemies" (qtd. in Boyer 6). Indeed, after the war ended, the atomic physicists were routinely portrayed as mystics emerging from the New Mexico desert with divine knowledge. In a clearly related incident, the *Enola Gay,* the plane from which the Hiroshima atomic bomb was dropped, was given divine blessing before take-off (Boyer 211). The holy "secret" supposedly behind the project fostered heightened security measures in the United States and was a central issue behind the Rosenberg Trial in the 1950s, as Stanley Goldburg has recently argued (51-52). Further, in his account of the Bikini Atoll tests of 1946, Bradley wrote in a manner typical of the theological mythologizing to which the Manhattan Project was subjected. Thus, after encountering a blackboard that had been used by Project physicists, he wrote: "Here, as there, enshrouded in darkness and barbed wire, the unknown scientists had come to work on their unmentionable discoveries, communicated in their strange language and hiero-glyphics, set up and conducted their experiments and then vanished, leaving only a scribbled note, 'The Manhattan District was here'" (142).

This view of atomic scientists as religious mystics comes forth most strongly in William Laurence's *Dawn Over Zero* (1946), which recounts the author's experiences with the Manhattan Project both at Trinity and in a plane over Nagasaki. Laurence describes the Trinity test in theologi-cal terms: "it was as though the earth had opened up and the skies had split. One felt as though one were present at the moment of creation when God said, 'Let there be light'" (10-11). The creation of the atomic bomb was an event that Laurence believed not to have "happened since Genesis" (163). Further, in a plane over Nagasaki, Laurence accepted his own potential death: "I found myself unperturbed by the thought. If this was to be my last [story], could anyone wish for a better?" (238). Citing Father Siemes, a Christian Missionary who lived in Hiroshima, Laurence callously remarks that the use of the bomb on Hiroshima "was a great boost for Christianity," because he had heard that it fostered more con-versions than those brought about "during the preceding long years" (248). Laurence's enthusiasm for the Atomic Age relied on a vision of a new world created by god-like physicists.

Manhattan-Project physicists also participated in the cultural mythologizing of their discoveries. The choice of Los Alamos for the Trinity Site deliberately situated the scientists in the site of the mystic—the desert—and that choice gave rise to views of the secret city as a mythical place. Ferenc Morton Szaz notes that local New Mexicans termed the site "'the Magic Mountain' or 'Shangri-La'" (17).[15] The sci-entists largely conceived of themselves as saviors who would end the war and usher in a new world of peace, roles, as Gar Alperovitz argues in his recent book on the creation of the atomic bomb, into which they were carefully drafted by U.S. military and government officials. Steal-ing their plot from H. G. Wells's 1914 novel *The World Set Free,* many Manhattan Project physicists believed that through their work they were going to be able to create a situation in which war would become so hor-rific that world peace would ensue.[16] Thus, Joseph O. Hirshfelder, a sci-entist at Los Alamos, argued that "the recruiting slogan of the Manhattan Project was 'Help win the war to end all wars,' and we felt that this was true. We thought that once World War II had been finished, wars would be much too horrible—there could never be another war, particularly if fearsome atomic energy was made available" (67-68). The primary insti-gator of this messianic purpose among the physicists was J. Robert Oppenheimer, the civilian coordinator of the Los Alamos site. The publi-cation of *One World or None* in 1946, a collection of essays by scientists, journalists, and military officials, was the manifesto of the physicists' messianic political movement, which lasted approximately from 1945-1950. The collection argues in favor of world government as the only means of preventing catastrophic nuclear war. In his representative contribution to the volume, Albert Einstein argued that only if atomic bombs were placed under international jurisdiction and a world government were formed could "we have some assurance that we shall not vanish into the atmosphere, dissolved into atoms, one of these days" (76).

In Lindner's account of physicist Kirk Allen, he mythologizes Allen's messianic purpose in his work at Los Alamos. Discussing Allen's professional life, Lindner says he rejects lobotomy and electro-shock "therapy," because Allen is "one of those valuable persons on whom the future of our civilization depends" (189). Further, Allen's brain houses information that is crucial both for individuals and for the human race as a whole (189). Lindner's valorization of Allen, who presumably is working on the H-bomb project at the time of the analysis, as a savior creates a problematic situation in which he is supposed to cure Allen of a messianic role in his delusional system while still affording him that role in 1950s society.

Allen's system, in which he is lord of a planet, is pervaded with the self-aggrandizement typical of the paranoiac. Allen's delusional system begins to be constructed when as a child he reads a work of fiction in which his own name coincides with the protagonist's name. Allen concludes that "*what I was reading was my own biography*" (171). Allen then begins to read most science fiction and fantasy works he encounters as part of his biography. Eventually, his creation of an elaborate alternative world allows him to live the adventures of an interplanetary savior who courts princesses, governs provinces, and battles enemies (172). Lindner speculates that Allen's attraction to atomic physics is due to the manner in which his fantasies and his research contain clear similarities (173). Certainly the Manhattan Project was viewed by many as a science-fiction project. Discussing the history of the project, Lawrence Badash observes that "more than once it appeared that nuclear efforts should be curtailed and the scientists' talents employed on less 'science fiction' type war projects" (xiv). Describing the experience of watching the bomb dropped on Nagasaki, Laurence comments that "what we saw made us feel that we were Buck Rogers twenty-fifth-century warriors" (219). A Buck Rogers-like character is what Allen becomes in his delusional system.

Allen the physicist, much like Schreber the would-be nerve doctor, is at pains to describe his system in scientific terms. The mass of physical evidence he creates to verify his system attests to this. Further, he attempts to theorize his journeys as produced by teleportation, "special physic equipment," a "unique organ," or "wild talent" (176). However, as was the case with Tausk's patients' mysterious machines and Schreber's transforming body, Allen cannot discover the clinching physical evidence. The secret of the paranoiac system remains mysterious, much as the "secret" of the atomic bomb is shrouded in mystery for non-physicists in postwar American society.

The question remains as to why Allen, a research physicist afforded respect and fame, should fall victim to paranoia. While I am not proposing to answer this question in any definitive manner, I want to suggest as a possibility Allen's need to construct an alternative world in which he participates in saving human lives, a need constructed in response to a reality in which he is responsible for working on a project that resulted in the deaths of hundreds of thousands of lives and by implication threatened to destroy the entire earth. Allen seeks to replace the scientific system that posits him as a god-destroyer with one in which he serves as a god-savior. While guilt was by no means an across-the-boards reaction on the part of the Manhattan Project scientists, it does characterize many scientists' reactions, Oppenheimer's being the most vocal. As Boyer summarizes, contemporary accounts and later reminiscences of Manhattan Project scientists suggest "that for many scientists involvement in the Manhattan Project was a traumatic experience that turned their lives inside-out" (49). Oppenheimer's statement to Truman that he believed he had blood on his hands and his view that the atomic scientists had known sin are responses, as Weart argues, to "the news from Hiroshima" (113). The personal accounts in *Reminiscences of Los Alamos* point to the varying levels of guilt and trauma experienced by those at Los Alamos. Elsie McMillan, wife of Los Alamos physicist Edwin M. McMillan, discusses the excessive drinking at Los Alamos parties, explaining "because you had to let off steam, you had to let off this feeling eating your soul, oh God are we doing right?" (43). McMillan was one of the few wives at Los Alamos who knew what work the physicists were doing in their secret city.[17] Richard Feynman discusses the trauma he experienced after returning to New York. Sitting at a restaurant in New York City, he was overcome by a vision of the city in ruins like Hiroshima. The repression of Hiroshima resulted in Feynman thinking "I would go along and I would see people building a bridge, or they'd be making a new road, and I thought, they're *crazy*, they just don't understand, they don't *understand*. Why are they making these new things? It's so useless" (132). Like trauma victims, some Manhattan Project scientists could not assimilate the unthinkable of Hiroshima and Nagasaki, and hence relived it, like Feynman, in traumatic scenes.[18]

The most horrific aspect of Hiroshima and Nagasaki was the most repressed aspect both culturally and individually—suffering bodies. Feynman's fear involves roads and bridges. Representations of the destruction of the two cities in the postwar period focused on ruins of buildings, scenes devoid of human bodies. Even John Hersey's *Hiroshima* (1946), which attempted to bring to the American public's attention the suffering involved in the destruction of this city, focused on the survivors. The United States government confiscated and banned (until 1968) a showing of actual footage shot in Hiroshima by Akira Iwasaki (Taylor 128). The U.S. military detained an Australian journalist, Wilfred Burchett, who photographed the aftermath in Hiroshima, and had his film and dispatch confiscated (Boyer 187). Even one of the most popularized fantasies of nuclear war occurring in the U.S., *Life* Magazine's "The 36-Hour War" (1945) shows nuclear holocaust occurring in the U.S. solely in terms of destroyed buildings. New York's Fifth Avenue is sketched in ruins, but the survivors tower over rubble, not human bodies (35). As Ellen Schrecker argues concerning postwar America, "just as the logic of the Cold War demanded a demonized and stereotyped enemy, so too it required an idealized American state, one that, by definition, could not possibly kill innocent people" (137). Today at the National Atomic Museum in Albuquerque, New Mexico, the film shown to visitors, "Ten Seconds That Shook the World" (1963), sanitizes the horror of the bombings of Hiroshima and Nagasaki by showing in Hiroshima only ruined buildings and by ignoring the issue of Nagasaki altogether. In his discussion of *Reminiscences of Los Alamos,* Bryan C. Taylor argues that the work atmosphere at Los Alamos created "atomized workers" who through their commitment to "technological innovation" were encouraged to withdraw psychically from the world (433). Taylor further notes that what characterizes many accounts in the collection is "a hegemonic conception of the bomb that was rhetorically derived from a structure that excluded the representation of human victims" (437).

The withdrawal from the immediate suffering world demanded of Los Alamos scientists and of the larger American public in the postwar years also describes one of the first symptoms of paranoia. As Freud's commentary on Schreber indicates, the first step toward paranoia is the withdrawal from the world on the part of the paranoiac: "the end of the world is the projection of this internal catastrophe; for his subjective world has come to an end since he has withdrawn his love from it" (146). The delusional world of the paranoiac is an attempt "*at recovery, a process of reconstruction*" (147). In Freud's theory, the paranoiac withdraws from the world (decathexis), directs his or her cathectic energy to the ego resulting in self-aggrandizement, and then attempts to reestablish a cathectic relationship with the world in the form of a delusional system. As Micheline Enriquez notes, "the paranoiac's 'insane' responses are always attempts at a cure, and attempt to situate themselves in relation to *an order* in which their identity would be assured" (106).

Lacan makes the connection between trauma and paranoia more clear as he discusses the paranoiac's delusions as representing that which is foreclosed by the Symbolic returning in the guise of the Imaginary, i.e., as hallucinations. The Real, which traumatizes the subject, returns in the paranoiac's system composed of delusions. The paranoiac, like the trauma victim, is attempting to represent the unrepresentable. Enriquez observes that the paranoiac, unlike the traumatized person, does not merely repeat the Real (the unrepresentable) but interprets it, thus attempting to "*graft sense upon non-sense, or to represent the un-representable*" (111). Thus the unrepresentable pain of Hiroshima and Nagasaki as part of the larger unrepresentability of atomic power returns in postwar American society in various guises both culturally and individually. Thus the giant ants, sea creatures, and other monsters in 1950s science-fiction films, the communist movement as demonic system as portrayed by McCarythism, and Kirk Allen's delusional universe all represent attempts to interpret the trauma of nuclear bombs.

While Lindner traces Allen's withdrawal from the world to his adolescent seduction by a governess, Allen's frequent tripping to his paranoiac universe occurs only while he is working at Los Alamos. Thus Allen relates that "one moment I was just a scientist on X Reservation bending over a drawing board in a clapboard B.Q. in the middle of an American desert—the next moment I was Kirk Allen, Lord of a planet in an interplanetary empire in a distant universe" (176). Allen's need for his alternative world heightens as he works on the atomic- and hydrogen-bomb projects. Further, when Lindner invades Allen's delusional world, feigning a belief in it that becomes real, he attempts to puncture the reality of the system by pointing to flaws in Allen's maps, flaws which lead Allen to speculate that his miscalculations have caused deaths. To Lindner's retort that the flaws are not serious, Allen responds, "not serious! why, man, these maps are used by my pilots. No wonder I've lost so many ships!" (191). Lindner reassures Allen that perhaps the maps they are examining are outdated while the pilots are following updated charts (192). Allen is reassured. What this episode illustrates is that like the myth of the necessity of the use of the atomic bombs on Japan that effaced suffering bodies in the postwar period, Allen's paranoiac system, when intact, effaces suffering and reassures him through its totality that he is a superhero, not a careless scientist who is responsible for human deaths.

The twist in Lindner's narrative lies in his conversion to Allen's system, a conversion that frees Allen from his delusional world. Lindner's increasing belief in Allen's system points to the contagious nature of paranoia, which is evident also in Freud's account in which Schreber's system impinges on Freud's, and Freud can no longer clarify which system is delusional and which is valid. Lindner "catches" Allen's paranoia, commenting that "with Kirk's puzzled assistance I was taking part in cosmic adventures, sharing the exhilaration of the sweeping extravaganza he had plotted" (201). Lindner traces his attraction to Allen's system back to his interest in science fiction (197) and to his interest in popularizations of cybernetics, higher mathematics, and astrophysics (198). Lindner, like Allen, like Schreber, and like Freud, is attracted to paranoia because it becomes a means of creating a perfect Newtonian system.

The doubts, trauma, and gaps that plague actual scientific systems, and have done so increasingly in the twentieth century, are effaced by the perfection of the paranoiac's system. Paranoia stands as a symptom of a culture that seeks complete answers in both its scientific discourse and in its technological capabilities. Mental patient, psychoanalyst, and physicist alike feel the powerful lure of paranoiac systems. As Lindner states apropos of Allen's system, "I had been attracted by the stupendous fantasy and felt, in myself, its magnetic pull . . ." (206). Perhaps as long as the siren song of Newtonian totalization is still heard, paranoia will continue to lure humans into a belief in its seductive, complete answers to complex issues.

In the following chapters, I trace paranoia as a means of both expressing and containing the trauma of nuclear weapons within 1950s sf films. What Kirk Allen lived on a delusional basis, many 1950s Americans experienced through cinematic representation. In a dangerous world of fall-out, medical experiments, and potential war, audiences found both comfort and terror in metaphorical embodiments of the frightening thing known as the Bomb. I begin this exploration by looking at the myths surrounding the atomic scientist himself.

2

THE ATOMIC SCIENTIST, SCIENCE FICTION FILMS, AND PARANOIA: *THE DAY THE EARTH STOOD STILL, THIS ISLAND EARTH,* AND *KILLERS FROM SPACE*

A commonplace of modern perceptions of the scientist is of him or her as a liminal figure, potentially hero, and potentially villain. In the popular imagination, the scientist who may cure ills and create utopian possibilities is also potentially the mad scientist bent on world destruction. Idealist Victor Frankenstein, transformed into an obsessed, monster-producing man, and Dr. Jekyll, transformed in the sanctity of his laboratory into Mr. Hyde, are two archetypal figures with whom modern scientists have been associated. The scientist as messiah figure bordering on apocalyptic destroyer partakes of the logic of paranoia. In postwar American society, heightened interest in the scientist focused on one particular type of scientist—the atomic scientist flush with the success of the Manhattan Project. Interest in the atomic scientist and cultural paranoia joined in both the "real" world of nuclear physics and in popular representations of the atomic scientist to reframe the savior/destroyer dichotomy within an Atomic Age in which the scientist literally did increasingly possess the ability to bring about apocalyptic destruction. The heyday of the atomic scientist as potential world-policy shaper extended from approximately 1945 to 1963, and sf continually explored the ramifications of the atomic scientist and his place in postwar American society. This chapter focuses on three sf films, *The Day the Earth Stood Still, This Island Earth,* and *Killers from Space,* which captured for the popular imagination ambivalences surrounding atomic scientists, ambivalences which were framed within a paranoiac discourse that characterized Manhattan Project scientists' portrayals of their mission to the postwar American public.

The messianic figures of Klaatu and Barnhardt in Robert Wise's *The Day the Earth Stood Still* (1951), Cal Meacham in Joseph Newman's *This Island Earth* (1954), and Doug Martin in W. Lee Wilder's *Killers from Space* (1954) may trace their lineage back to Daniel Paul Schreber. Schreber presented himself as a messiah for a new world order. He believed that God had chosen him to be the mother of a new race of humans following a world catastrophe in which he was the only human spared. Schreber believed that rays were transforming his body into a female one. He wrote of the singularity of his experience: "in fact since the dawn of the world there can hardly have been a case like mine," commenting on his contact with departed human souls and with God (88-89). As messiah, Schreber was given revelations into the workings of God and the Order of the World, revelations that no human had experienced before. Schreber stated that he "had to solve one of the most intricate problems ever set for man and . . . [he] had to fight a sacred battle for the greatest good of mankind" (130). Schreber had not only to propagate a new human species, but also had to fight for the protection of the Earth itself; for example, he believed he traveled to Brazil to build a wall protecting heaven against a yellow flood that he took to be a syphilis epidemic (87).

Curiously, while Schreber's delusions point to the self-aggrandizement typical of paranoiac discourse, they also reveal him as the culprit behind the destruction of human life on Earth.[1] Schreber was the solution to the threatened extinction of the human species, but he was also its cause. He commented that God threatens to destroy the human race because he knows that increased nervousness on Earth can endanger his existence (56). Human nervousness can result in a serious danger that impinges on God's realms (57-58). God is drawn to Earth because he perceives nervousness there reaching dangerous levels, and the chief culprit in this increased nervous energy was Schreber himself. His "over-excited nerves" had summoned God to Earth to destroy it, because his nervousness exceeded any which had previously existed (119). Like Victor Frankenstein making the creature and then assuming the role of savior of the world from its danger, Schreber's messianic role resulted from an apocalypse for which he himself had been largely responsible.

This same tension between destroyer and savior is visible in both the political discourse written by Manhattan Project scientists and in 1950s sf representations of these scientists. The creation of the atomic bomb is a complicated and multi-layered story. As Gar Alperovitz's study of the Manhattan Project emphasizes, although some scientists were vocal in their desire to appeal for modifications in the use of the atomic bombs on Japan, appealing for a demonstration without Japanese casualties, for example, the scientist "had virtually no impact on government decisions" (185).[2] The Chicago branch of the Project, led by Leo Szilard, submitted a petition to Truman, but as Alperovitz concludes, it was most likely never even read by the President (191).

Moreover, in the fever-paced atmosphere of the heart of the Los Alamos branch, scientists who thoughtfully considered ethical implications of the creation of the atomic bomb were few and far between. Manhattan Project scientists were recruited into the project with the purpose of creating an atomic bomb before Germany did. Einstein's famous 1939 letter to Roosevelt put forth the proposition that salved the consciences of most scientists: build an atomic bomb before the Nazis do. John H. Manley, one of Oppenheimer's aides at Los Alamos, underscores the important purpose the scientists at Los Alamos felt they possessed: "our task was to pursue a development to resolve a conflict of half the world" (32). As George B. Kistiakowsky (chief of the explosives division at Los Alamos) makes clear, military propaganda staved off ethical discussions of the implications of the project: "there was no organized movement at Los Alamos to stop the bomb use. I changed my mind afterwards but I was very much influenced by the military estimate of what would happen that summer" (64). Kistiakowsky's comment highlights the perception on the part of the scientists that even after the surrender of Germany, bomb production had to continue: the propaganda projected extreme casualties which were discounted by the U.S. Strategic Bombing Survey in 1946, but which (as Alperovitz's study makes clear) have continued to haunt popular perceptions of the use of the atomic bombs on Japan.[3] Joseph O. Hirschfelder, group leader in the Ordnance and Theoretical Divisions at Los Alamos, comments on the messianic purpose which fueled continued work on the bomb: "the recruiting slogan of the Manhattan project was 'Help win the war to end all wars,' and we felt that this was true. We thought that once World War II had been finished, war would be much too horrible—there could never be another war, particularly if fearsome atomic energy was made available" (67-68). And then while building their weapons, the scientists began to perceive themselves as potential saviors—an image largely fueled by J. Robert Oppenheimer. This view lay behind the short-lived scientists' movement and was a view which sf films continued to promote in the postwar period. This self-fashioned image of the atomic scientists is one that has continued to be held by some of the scientists involved in the project. In a 1995 interview, Hans Bethe repeated the original propaganda: "the third alternative, the atomic bomb, caused horrible destruction in the two cities of Hiroshima and Nagasaki, but for Japan as a whole it was the lesser evil. It meant far fewer deaths and less destruction than blockade or invasion would have meant. It convinced Emperor Hirohito to surrender and ended the war" (qtd. in Conners 43). Bethe made no mention of the fact that is now well known that Japan was making motions to surrender at the time the bombs were dropped.

Like the scientists' movement, sf films enact a fantasy of the atomic scientist as the most important figure in American society. While atomic scientists in reality had little impact on the political sphere, in *The Day the Earth Stood Still,* they bring about a radical change in U.S. policy. Thus Klaatu's powers allow him to threaten the U.S. government and military with destruction if they do not adopt peaceful uses of atomic power. Although Dr. Barnhardt is initially marginalized, his association with Klaatu allows him to help dictate American policy. In *This Island Earth* and *Killers from Space,* the scientists Cal Meacham and Doug Martin literally hold the fate of America and the entire world in their hands as they uncover alien take-over schemes. Whereas atomic scientists may have had little or no impact on public policy, sf, like the scientists' movement, afforded a forum whereby they were granted the illusion of a god-like power over human existence.

The messianic purpose of the atomic scientists found its best expression in *One World or None.* The articles in this collection and other articles published by and about atomic scientists in the immediate postwar period portray atomic scientists as mystics who impart political and ethical wisdom to a frightened American public. These discussions of future atomic-war scenarios were created with the purpose of initiating a world government and promoting international nuclear-weapons control, but their discursive strategy was the promotion of a frightening paranoiac vision of the Atomic Age. In his discussion of the Manhattan Project, William L. Laurence portrays the atomic scientists as messiahs emerging from the New Mexico desert, an image that was picked up frequently in postwar accounts of the Project. After watching the Trinity Test, Laurence believes he has witnessed a new Genesis (10-11). Laurence views the Project scientists as men who literally hold the godlike power of life and death over the entire world: "used properly, it [atomic power] gives man the means for realizing the dream of the ages. With it he can shatter his world to bits 'and then remould it nearer to the Heart's Desire.' Or he can just shatter it to bits" (20). An article in the *St. Louis Post-Dispatch* from 1945 articulates a similar view of the scientists as either saviors or destroyers: "either the world's people—our own included—will learn to use it not for war but peace, or else science has signed the mammalian world's death warrant and deeded an earth in ruins to the ants." In a 1946 article, "Gentlemen: You Are Mad!" Lewis Mumford views the Atomic Age as an age of madmen, because the authority figures "have been carrying through a series of acts which will lead eventually to the destruction of mankind, under the solemn conviction that they are normal responsible people, living sane lives, and working for reasonable ends" (5). Mumford looks to the scientists as the only hope of salvation from the madmen: although the scientists are "the greatest of the madmen" because they invented the bomb, they "in the final throes of their dementia, were shocked back into sanity" (5). Like Mumford, the Project scientists presented themselves as offering the only panacea against world destruction.

The Day the Earth Stood Still, This Island Earth, and *Killers from Space* also offer the scientist as the only hope for the continuation of human civilization. Klaatu travels to Earth to offer it a last chance to create a peaceful world before its policies force other planets to destroy its war-mongering citizens. Cal Meacham and Doug Martin serve as detective-scientists who uncover plots on the part of alien cultures to take over America. In these three films, as in the scientists' movement, only the atomic scientist possesses the intelligence and sensitivity to save the Earth from its own and other planets' destructive tendencies. The paranoia present in representation in these films allegorizes the paranoia of the scientists' movement.

The creation of the scientists' movement after the use of atomic bombs on Japan partook of the theological and self-aggrandizing delusions of paranoia. Describing Oppenheimer's creation of The Federation of Atomic Scientists, Hirschfelder comments:

on a cold, rainy Sunday night in the winter of 1945, Oppenheimer assembled most of the Los Alamos scientists in a small wooden chapel, and, between claps of lightening, explained how all of us would live our lives in fear, but how fear itself might be responsible for maintaining peace until at long last all of the nations had learned to settle their differences in a reasonable manner. (70)

The promotion of fear of apocalyptic destruction and the either/or binary logic that characterizes paranoia informs the articles that make up the bible of the scientists' movement, *One World or None.*[4]

One World or None seeks to frighten its audience with the inevitable horrific outcome of atomic bombs if a world government is not formed and if nuclear weapons are not put under international control. Arthur Compton's introduction to the collection sets up the either/or logic that lies behind the rhetorical strategies of the scientists' movement. Compton argues that either wars will be outlawed by international agreement or "catastrophic conflict" will result (v). The atomic scientists contributing to this collection fashion themselves as saviors, as the promoters of the peaceful atom, and portray the nation state as the demonic force that may bring about world destruction.

The division of the world into heroes and villains characterizes the paranoiac worldview, and this is also the view *One World* promotes. In his contribution to the volume, Niels Bohr predicts a nuclear holocaust that will outstrip the imagination in its extremity: "the grim realities being revealed to the world these days will no doubt, in the minds of many, revive the terrifying prospects forecast in fiction" (ix-x). Bohr implies that sf has been a prophetic voice in presenting the potential horrors of atomic bombs.[5] Philip Morrison imagines the destruction of New York City through atomic bombs and reminds the audience that "your city, too, is a good target" (3). Oppenheimer's contribution to the volume informs the audience that atomic power is "revolutionary" because it promises "rapid technological change" and "fantastic powers of destruction" (22), concluding that world government offers the only security for the United States (25). In another article published in 1946, Oppenheimer labels the atomic bomb "an evil thing" (7), but argues that the evil can be made good by presenting "an opportunity unique and challenging" to create world peace (9). Our potential destruction can be converted into our salvation in Oppenheimer's view, a view that dominates the scientists' movement. The only contributor to the volume more prestigious than Oppenheimer is Einstein. In his article, Einstein promotes fear by stating that if world government and international nuclear control do not come about we may "vanish into the atmosphere, dissolved into atoms, one of these days" (76). In an article published in *The Atlantic Monthly*, Einstein directly states that fear is the only means of achieving the political goals of the scientists' movement: "since I do not foresee that atomic energy is to be a great boon for a long time, I have to say that for the present it is a menace. Perhaps it is well that it should be. It may intimidate the human race into bringing order into its international affairs, which, without the pressure of fear, it would not do" (45).

The black-and-white moral outlook that characterizes paranoiac discourse and the scientists' movement's promotion of fear finds expression in subsequent sf films.[6] In Wise's film, Klaatu's messianic mission is opposed by stereotypical representations of a war-mongering military, xenophobic citizens (represented by the inhabitants of the boarding house), and an amoralistic publicity seeker (Tom Stevens). Heroic Americans (Helen Benson, Bobby Benson, and Dr. Barnhardt) who defy prejudice and recognize a messiah when they see one aid Klaatu. Norman Cameron theorizes paranoia as relying upon a pseudo-community of villains that is complemented by a pseudo-community of friends. Cameron comments, "what he [the paranoiac] takes to be a functional community is only a pseudo-community created by his own unskilled attempts at interpretation, anticipation, and validation of social behavior" ("Pseudo-Community" 37). The pseudo-community of enemies in *The Day the Earth Stood Still* consists of politicians, the military, and businessmen, whereas the pseudo-community of friends, the element that complements the enemies and reinforces the black-and-white morality of paranoia (Cameron, "Revisited" 56), is composed of scientists, women, and children. Similarly, in *This Island Earth,* Cal Meacham can find support for his suspicions about Exeter only in the other good American scientists, Ruth Adams and Steve Carlson, who, unlike their international colleagues, resist co-option into the Metalunan plan to colonize the Earth. Further, Neutron the cat becomes part of Meacham's pseudo-community of friends as it alerts him to the monitoring function of the interocitor. Both *The Day the Earth Stood Still* and *This Island Earth* create pseudo-communities of friends who sentimentalize the scientist's status as messiah figure. If women, children, and animals sympathize with the scientist's plight, then he must be morally irreproachable. While Doug Martin in *Killers from Space* has no community of friends to affirm his rightness, the fact that he is able single-handedly to resist the mind control attempted by the aliens and then save the Earth from alien takeover highlights his status as super-scientist. The fact that these scientists must operate outside of the channels of traditional authority structures points to another concern that both the scientists' movement and sf films explore.

Several contributors to *One World or None* worry about the United States turning into a police state in the name of national security. Paradoxically, the scientists' movement helped promote McCarthyism by creating a paranoiac world vision that would be appropriated by McCarthy and HUAC (House Un-American Activities Committee) to justify coercion and suppression. E. U. Condon warns of "the police state, which must result from this hard fact [atomic power] in a world from which war has not yet been banished!" (40). Irving Langmuir warns of the threat to civil liberties posed by HUAC (52). While the scientists' movement received national support and respect from 1945 through 1949, the Soviet explosion of an atomic bomb in 1949 fostered the shifting mood toward the promotion of national security and away from a desire for world government and international control. In 1951, Eugene Rabinowitch concluded (in *The Bulletin of the Atomic Scientists*) that the scientists' movement had failed because through its promotion of fear, it encouraged reliance on atomic weapons rather than abolition and/or control of them: "while trying to frighten men into rationality, scientists have frightened many into abject fear or blind hatred" (12). Paul Boyer concludes that "the scientists' manipulation of fear, rather than the particular causes they espoused, seems their principal legacy. Indeed, they may have served as unwitting advance agents of the very anti-Communist hysteria most of them deplored" (106). By 1952, when Philip Morrison, an atomic scientist and contributor to *One World,* wrote a review of a book by British author P. M. S. Blackett that espoused views similar to those expressed in *One World,* he was called before a congressional anti-Communist investigating committee, and his 1949 review of the book was used as "evidence" of his communist sympathies (*Subversive* 1952). As Bruce Robbins argues in a recent article, the Rosenbergs were executed for enacting the agenda of the scientists' movement: "to take [knowledge of the bomb] out of the control of any one nation—including our own" (144).

Seen within this climate, a 1951 film that continues to promote the political agenda of the scientists' moment might be viewed as extraordinary, yet *The Day the Earth Stood Still* uses a scientist, Klaatu, from another galaxy to promote the now very unpopular and suspect views of the scientists' movement to a large sf audience. Like *One World or None,* Wise's film uses a paranoiac framework to fight the paranoia of HUAC. Klaatu arrives in Washington, D.C., to find himself in the midst of a national (in)security state. The landing of the spacecraft is immediately perceived as a threat. Troops surround the spaceship, pointing weapons at it for two hours. Although Klaatu emerges promising peace and good will, a soldier shoots him anyway, resulting in the emergence of the robot Gort from the ship.[7] Klaatu's promise of peace could not be read at face value in 1951, due to "the Aesopian language thesis" adopted in the *Dennis v. United States* decision that year. This theory argued that "communist language was hardly ever meant literally . . . if Dennis produced a text which claimed 'peace' as the communists' objective, it was to be read as intending 'war'" (Filreis 307). The fact that Klaatu is suspected of being a communist is made manifest in the film when Mrs. Barley expresses her fear that the spaceman has come from the Soviet Union. The soldier who shoots him hence reads Klaatu's promise of peace as potentially meaning war, and indeed the soldier is proven right. Klaatu comes to Earth to threaten destruction of the planet if it extends its aggressions into outer space via atomic-powered rockets.

Adopting the scientists' movement's perspective, the film portrays the nation state as a ridiculous, outdated concept. Klaatu refuses to address one nation. The president's representative, Harley, attempts to explain Cold War politics to Klaatu, but he labels it a "petty squabble," and tells Harley, "I'm impatient with stupidity." Klaatu represents a paranoiac vision from the viewpoint of the scientists' movement. He is a more highly evolved powerful messiah figure who comes to the Earth to foist the scientists' agenda on the world with a force that cannot be denied.[8] Like Schreber's delusion that he has been chosen to save the human race, *The Day the Earth Stood Still* represents the grand delusion of the scientists' movement, that a higher power supports their views and will help enact them in a U.S. that is becoming increasingly nationalistic and driven by paranoiac fantasy. Thus this sf film promotes a paranoiac solution to the problem of the McCarthyist paranoiac reality.

The direct connection the film makes back to the scientists' movement is through the character of Dr. Barnhardt, a character who, as a contemporary review notes, Sam Jaffe plays "with an Einstein hair-do" ("New Pictures" 100). While Einstein had represented the very epitome of the adored scientist, by 1951 his status was becoming increasingly suspect. Peter Biskind notes that *The Day the Earth Stood Still* "was crawling far out on a very thin limb" by extolling Einstein (153). In 1945 Einstein was attacked by a HUAC member, John Rankin, for being an "agitator," and his status as potential Communist continued in the 1950s. Wise's film, however, venerates Einstein in the character of Barnhardt. Bobby tells Klaatu that Barnhardt is the smartest man in the world. Barnhardt protects Klaatu from government agents, and Klaatu praises him by telling him, "you have faith." Barnhardt expresses disillusionment over the failed scientists' movement, telling Klaatu, "we scientists are too often ignored or misunderstood." Klaatu's ability to stop all electrically-powered machinery on Earth for half an hour gives the world's scientists new political power. Barnhardt is pleased by the fear Klaatu's display instills in his maid: "[D]oes all this frighten you? Does this make you feel insecure? Good, Hilda, I'm glad!" The meeting called by Barnhardt witnesses Klaatu's resurrection and the warning he gives to the world.

Paradoxically, the film suggests that the only force possible to battle the McCarthyist police state is one provided by an interplanetary police state. Klaatu tells his audience that Gort and the other robot policemen "have absolute power over us" in matters of aggression, a point that Harry Bates' story, on which the film is based, makes even more clear when the robot (there named Gnut) reveals to the protagonist that "I am the master" (179). Klaatu's message partakes of the same paranoiac either/or logic as *One World or None* does: "join us and live in peace or pursue your present course and face obliteration." While *The Day the Earth Stood Still* enacts an sf paranoiac vision of the scientists' movement ultimately succeeding in American politics, it presents the vexed solution of the substitution of an interplanetary police state promising "security for all" for the national (in)security state of McCarthyist America.[9] While Wise's film seems to accept the scientist as a savior figure (extolling Klaatu as Christ-like and Barnhardt as a faithful disciple) other 1950s sf films explore the slippage between villain and hero that characterized many postwar perceptions of the atomic scientist.

This Island Earth deals with the scientist as superstar who is easily lured into working for the Metalunans as they attempt to defend their war-torn planet. Cal Meacham, the scientist protagonist, is first seen in the film being photographed by reporters. He tells them that he is working for the peaceful atom and displays his naiveté by touting his "peaceful" work while flying back to Los Angeles in a private Air Force jet. Cal's celebrity status results in the Metalunans saving him when his jet goes out of control and sending him an interocitor to assemble as a kind of an entrance exam before initiating him into the Metalunans' laboratory work in Georgia. Interestingly, the Metalunans have put Cal's jet out of control in the first place: thus, not knowing this, he is trapped into working for them out of a sense of gratitude. The film highlights Cal's science-for-science's sake attitude which allows him to be seduced by the Metalunans' scientific project and raises ethical questions about the dangers of the "objective," amoral scientist which many recent commentators on the ethics of science have been raising.[10]

On one level the film may be viewed as allegorizing the fear that communists can easily dupe the atomic scientist. The Rosenberg Trial along with the 1950 revelation of Klaus Fuchs' transmission of information from Los Alamos to the Soviet Union had made the American people hypersensitive regarding possible leaks within the scientific community. Thus Klaus Fuchs represented the heroic atomic scientist transformed into a villain, and this potential fate is implied for Cal as well. The fact that the Metalunans choose Georgia as the site for their research lab suggests connections with the USSR, since Georgia is the one state name that was common to both the US and the USSR. The heightened security at the plantation house with the panopticon-like world created by the interocitor recalls paranoiac postwar views of a Soviet Union in which everyone is under surveillance. The fact that Exeter lures the scientists in with the promise of peace again suggests the "Aesopian language thesis" that informed anti-Communist paranoia.

Raymond F. Jones' novella (on which the film is based) brings out more explicitly the suspicion on the part of Cal and the other scientists that they have been duped into working for the Soviets. Cal's assistant, Joe Wilson, asks him if the interocitor may not be "some sort of Trojan Horse gadget" (195), referencing the so-called Trojan Horse strategy described by Harry and Bonaro Overstreet in their anti-Communist book as a ploy whereby the American Communist Party "abruptly abandoned its former revolutionary line—so far as public appearances were concerned—and began to call itself a 'progressive' American Party" (7-8). Joe fears that they are building a "gadget"—Los Alamos slang for an atomic bomb—for the Soviets. In Jones' novella, Cal tells Ruth that "because this place is so close to the engineering paradise I've always dreamed about I don't want to get kicked out for going around asking the top guys if they've signed loyalty pledges" (215). Cal suggests that even if he were working for the Soviets it would not bother him, because of the extraordinary conditions he finds in the lab under which to conduct his research. While Cal in the film is immediately suspicious of Exeter and the project he and the other scientists are working on, rejecting Exeter's use of peace to foster his work, Cal in the novella is taken in by the project and only when coerced by Ruth does he recognize that the scientists are being used by the Metalunans.[11]

While *This Island Earth* is registering paranoia about a Soviet Union that can control scientists' minds and create a panopticon-like environment in which the Soviets are "milking our scientific genius for all they can" (210), the work may be as likely allegorizing the Manhattan Project itself, presenting the paranoiac view of a United States police state expressed in the work of postwar commentators like Lewis Mumford. Like the propaganda behind the Manhattan Project, Exeter's propaganda uses the ultimate goal of ending war altogether to recruit support for his project on the part of the scientists. In Newman's film, Exeter tells Cal to have faith in "our ultimate aims." In the novella, Cal is seduced by the nukespeak "Peace Engineers," a term which designates the scientists at the laboratory, because he is told by Jorgasnovara (Exeter's character's name in the novella) that his organization "kept the atomic bomb from being used in the First World War instead of the Second" (217). In Jones' novella, the connection between the laboratory and Los Alamos is made more explicit as it is located in the American Southwest. From this perspective, the paranoiac fantasy of an always-watching interocitor can be read as fear of an American police state in which scientists have been lured into working on the atomic bomb project, and then find themselves trapped into government work and surveillance in the interest of national security. As I discuss later, Oppenheimer's loss of his security clearance in 1954 indicated the rhetorical trap the atomic scientist found himself in if he attempted to oppose weapon development.

In his 1954 collection of essays, *In the Name of Sanity*, Lewis Mumford captures the paranoiac discourse of one who fears not communist infiltration but an American McCarthyist police state. Mumford portrays postwar America as a place "where reason is cowed by governmental purges and subverted by irrational measures for counteracting subversion; where criticism and dissent and even normal human error are identified as treason" (7). Mumford portrays the United States government as an organization that has duped scientists into becoming mass murderers. This view was also expressed in a letter written to *Time* in 1945 that labeled the United States as "the new masters of brutality, infamy, atrocity" because "Bataan, Buchenwald, Dachau, Coventry,

Lidice were tea parties compared with the horror which we, the people of the United States of America, have dumped on the world in the form of atomic energy bombs" (W. Taylor). When Cal realizes that Exeter has fooled him into working on weapons for a war the Metalunans are fighting against their enemy, he accuses Exeter of mass murder. In Jones' novella, Cal is horrified to realize that as a Peace Engineer he has been serving a war machine: "these Peace Engineers—what a ghastly joke their name turned out to be! They have become involved in full-scale war" (232). *This Island Earth* may be seen as allegorizing the plight of "objective" scientists who were easily fooled into working on a project with which many later regretted becoming involved. Kistiakowsky expresses regret that military propaganda convinced scientists to keep working on the bomb because "the feeling was conveyed to us that Japan was very far from surrender, that the war could continue for a long time" (65). In the film, Cal receives information about the interocitor on a piece of paper with no letterhead. During the 1950s, the FBI typically conveyed information in the form of "blind memoranda," which were "typed on plain, unwatermarked paper that gave no evidence of its origins" (Schrecker 2).

While *This Island Earth* may be viewed as allegorizing the Manhattan Project and the ethical questions resulting from the construction and use of atomic bombs, it presents this topic in typically a paranoiac framework as does Wise's film. In his analysis of Schreber's memoirs, Freud discusses paranoia as operating according to the mechanism of "decomposition." Paranoia duplicates and distributes a single relationship into many, whereas hysteria condenses (125). In terms of sf's particular relationship to paranoia, it can be said that sf, like Schreber's *Memoirs,* extends earthly concerns into interplanetary duplication. Concerns of this world, of postwar America, become replicated and projected onto the whole universe. Commenting on Schreber, Allen S. Weiss notes that "the paranoiac mechanism strives to assume the greatest possibility of disjunctions and recombinations" (81). It is the language of science fiction that Schreber uses to distribute his personal conflicts throughout the universe. Schreber theorizes God populating planets through entering a corpse and absorbing the nerves (51); he postulates parallel worlds, commenting on a mirror Poland that exists somewhere in the universe (74n); he discusses the possibility of humans possessing vague recollections of their earlier existences on other planets (51). What I am suggesting *vis-à-vis* the three sf films under discussion here is that they distribute postwar concerns over McCarthyism, communism, and atomic power throughout the universe, making the paranoia of postwar America a universal concept. Thus in *This Island Earth,* scientists are not under surveillance by just the U.S. and/or the U.S.S.R, but by beings on other planets, the Metalunans in the novel, an interplanetary federation in the novella.

Due to the heightened importance of the scientist in this paranoiac vision, his role as messiah becomes even more prominent. In *This Island Earth,* as in Schreber's *Memoirs,* the savior figure is also the figure who calls forth the alien power. Cal's scientific expertise and the world's new-found knowledge of atomic power draw the Metalunans to Earth, which can now help them produce the needed radiation to defend their planet. Not only does Cal's celebrity status and scientific knowledge force him to work for the purposes of war, but the Metalunans plan to colonize Earth when their planet is eventually destroyed. Cal fights this idea and eventually convinces Exeter to allow him and Ruth to return home alone. Seeing the Earth he has saved single-handedly from alien invasion, Cal comments, "thank God it's still here." In Jones' novella, the messianic role of Cal is much more powerful than it is in the film. There, the Earth's production plants result in the Earth being targeted for destruction by the federation's enemies. Jorgasnovara explains to Cal that Earth is expendable and does so through an analogy made between Earth and a "primitive" place on earth during World War II: "you have had experience during your own recent World War. You saw how the waves of battle washed back and forth over primitive peoples who had little or no comprehension of who was fighting, or to what purpose" (247). In Jorgasnovara's view, Earth is a "primitive" planet because, as he tells Cal, "your people were barely out of caves when it [the inter-planetary war] began" (247). Cal travels to the federation to plead for defense of Earth, and wins the Federation over. Cal becomes the savior of the entire planet, a planet he and other scientists have put in danger due to their experimentation with atomic power.

While *This Island Earth* enacts the paranoiac split between savior/destroyer that plagued perceptions of the atomic scientist, a low-budget film from the same year enacts the paranoiac fantasy of atomic-scientist-as-hero who at any moment may mutate into world-destroyer. This is *Killers from Space,* which was released the same year that Oppenheimer lost his security clearance, and while the film is not based on Oppenheimer's trial, both *Killers from Space* and the Oppenheimer issue highlight the slippage from hero to villain that endangered the postwar atomic scientist, both in reality and in representation. As David Halberstam notes, by 1952 Oppenheimer was identified by a *Wall Street Journal* article as a "bad scientist" for opposing the development of the hydrogen bomb. In 1953 *Fortune* magazine published a piece that fingered Oppenheimer as a man who wanted to "reverse US military strategy" (342). Even prior to his security clearance hearings, the press was transforming Oppenheimer from hero into villain.

Doug Martin is clearly based on Oppenheimer, who represented the atomic scientist *par excellence* for the American public. Doug smokes a pipe as did Oppenheimer, wears a hat similar to one worn by Oppenheimer in famous photographs from Los Alamos, and is described as a workaholic who played "a key role in the planning of these operations [bomb tests]." Like Cal Meacham, the aliens choose Doug because of his superior knowledge: he is the most famous and the most visible of nuclear scientists and hence attracts the alien invaders.

Heroic, Oppenheimer-like Doug Martin is killed in a plane crash during a bomb test at Nevada while he is attempting to take radiation measurement from the cloud, and then he is resurrected as a zombie in the service of the aliens. The alien spaceship draws Doug's plane into the mushroom cloud, and it crashes, but Doug's body disappears. When he returns to the military base, he has a scar on his chest and is immediately under suspicion by Briggs, the FBI man brought in to investigate Doug's disappearance. Briggs introduces the possibility of Doug having been replaced by an impostor. The suspicion cast on Doug results in him losing his security privileges and being labeled by Colonel Banks as a "security risk." *Killers from Space* charts the mutation of a top atomic scientist into a zombie in the service of aliens who wish to colonize Earth. The shift in valence from hero to villain in the case of Doug Martin strikingly resembles the rhetorical transformation of Oppenheimer from patriot into "security risk" that characterized his 1954 trial.

Rachel L. Holloway's study of the Oppenheimer issue charts the demonization of the U.S.'s most famous scientist, which was enacted with the designation of Oppenheimer as a "security risk" in 1954. A central issue in the Oppenheimer trial was his vocal opposition to the development of the hydrogen bomb. As Holloway notes, Oppenheimer's former connections to the Communist Party were well known when he took over as civilian director of Los Alamos: "twice, in 1943 and 1947, Oppenheimer had received security clearance in spite of this information. Nevertheless, in 1954, the very same evidence led to his dismissal" (10). Thus Oppenheimer was portrayed as opposing "progress" because of his opposition to the H-bomb: in the public's mind, as Holloway argues, "he had come to stand in the way of the very thing he had represented for most citizens" (104-05).[12] In the popular press, Oppenheimer was transformed from messianic "father of the bomb," into "the potential 'scientist villain'" (25).

In the film, Doug's transformation is a similar one. His interest in studying radiation levels in the test makes him suspect, as he is potentially questioning the safety of atmospheric testing. His "weakness," his lack of faith in "progress" calls forth the aliens who control his mind and use him as a tool for the destruction of the Earth's population by giant animals and insects. It is Doug's invention, the A-bomb, which both summons the aliens and makes them strong. The aliens accumulate the energy released with bomb tests to fuel their mind-controlling rays. As with Cal Meacham and Schreber, Doug, in the paranoiac view of the film, has summoned the aliens because of his unique powers.

Unlike Oppenheimer, however, Doug is able to "redeem" himself, to clear the suspicions cast on him by the FBI by saving the Earth from the aliens. Doug shuts the electric power station off and destroys the aliens in an atomic explosion as the stored energy backfires on them. Doug and his wife, Ellen, look out the power-station window and are now comforted by the mushroom cloud, whereas before it troubled Doug as he conducted tests of the radiation levels. As in most paranoiac visions, *Killers from Space* achieves a closure that the issue of Oppenheimer's security clearance could not. Edward Jaye, discussing the similarities between fiction and paranoia, comments that "like paranoia, fiction diminishes anxiety through its emphasis upon objective problems which can be dealt with more effectively. External hopes and fears supplant an internal confusion which otherwise seems insoluble" (143). The difficult ethical issues raised by Oppenheimer and the other atomic scientists who opposed weapons research are resolved in *Killers from Space* through the external agency of the aliens. Doug's doubt about the bomb is seen as summoning forth the aliens who threaten the Earth with destruction. When Doug learns to gaze admiringly at the mushroom cloud, his questionable loyalty is resolved into patriotic support of "progress."

Both the scientists' movement and sf representations of the atomic scientist partook of paranoiac discourse to battle the perceived threat of postwar McCarthyism and isolationism to personal liberties and world peace. Commentators like Lewis Mumford underscore the contagious quality of a paranoiac worldview. As Freud "catches" Schreber's paranoia in the course of his commentary on the *Memoirs,* perceiving striking similarities between his discourse and Schreber's, those who sought to oppose the arms race either through political action or representation appropriated paranoiac discourse to further their progressive ends. In the scientists' movement and in sf films, the atomic scientist is granted a centrality he simply did not possess in the realpolitik of postwar America. As potential savior/destroyer, the scientist assumes a prominence that elides the other political and cultural forces behind the use of atomic bombs and the arms race. As such, the postwar atomic scientist, fashioned after nineteenth-century models such as Victor Frankenstein, provides a site where difficult ethical questions are replaced by a lone individual who bears both the blame and the praise for the double-edged continuation of scientific "progress."

What is the true dark side of the progress represented by the atomic bomb? The main postwar answer has been—radiation. The atomic scientist may have been perceived as a messiah on one level, but on another level he introduced a horrible new substance into American life, one which could contaminate and *invade* the human body. The next chapter explores the metaphorical dimensions of this invasion.

3

THE INVADED BODY:
PARANOIA AND RADIATION ANXIETY
IN *INVADERS FROM MARS,*
IT CAME FROM OUTER SPACE,
AND *INVASION OF THE BODY SNATCHERS*

One repressed aspect of atomic paranoia in 1950s America is radiation contamination.[1] Although propaganda policies attempted to allay public fear of radiation fallout through emphasis on the safety of bomb shelters and on the sunny side of the atom, examination of science fiction films of the 1950s reveals paranoiac structures arising from a fear of a United States increasingly contaminated by radiation and by the misinformation structures which sought to conceal this danger. Within the larger category of alien-invasion films of the 1950s, a subgenre is discernible which deals with the internal invasion of the human body by an alien force. In this chapter I focus on three 1950s sf classics, *Invaders from Mars, It Came from Outer Space,* and *Invasion of the Body Snatchers,* as manifestations of paranoiac structures that reveal postwar anxieties regarding radiation, gender, and sexuality.

The imperceptibly altered body is a staple of the paranoiac world. Within Schreber's paranoiac system he perceived himself surrounded by replicant humans he termed "fleeting-improvised men," creatures who resemble ordinary humans but who, in his view, were souls put down temporarily on earth by divine miracle. Schreber increasingly saw himself as one of the sole humans left on earth due to an unspecified world catastrophe, while the purpose of the improvised men was to provide for him the necessities of life until the transformed Schreber could renew the human race. Schreber argued that he had a special ability to recognize these improvised men that no one else possessed. While in Flechsig's asylum, Schreber saw himself surrounded "not by real people but by miraculously created puppets" (42-43n). During the latter part of his stay in the asylum, Schreber believed that he was the only real human left alive; the others who surrounded him were improvised men (85). Schreber found evidence for his theory of the replicant humans in an incident in which he saw an asylum attendant who slept in his room "becoming one with his bed": further, this same attendant occasionally dressed in Schreber's clothes in order to sustain the illusion of humanity (104). Schreber's paranoiac world was one in which humans looked the same outwardly, but were not human at all.

Further, Schreber's *Memoirs* chronicle the invasion of his body by the divine rays of God, an invasion that was unmanning him. Schreber argued that rays were invading his body in order to transform him into a woman. While he feared that God was unmanning him in order to transform him into a whore, he believed the Order of the World, to which God was subject, was unmanning him in order to make him the mother of a new race after a world catastrophe had depopulated the earth. Schreber thought that the rays were resulting in his penis retracting into his body and being changed into female sexual organs; simultaneously his skin and skeletal structure were becoming female (77n). In order to effect his transformation, God also placed scorpions in Schreber's brain that were to destroy his mental capacities (99). Schreber's body was becoming a fully invaded site as souls entered his body in the forms of three-millimeter men, jelly-like nerves, and talking rays. Schreber had his internal organs destroyed, restored, and replaced with different organs. While Schreber placed faith in the Order of the World, he was tormented by the process of unmanning that the rays were bringing about: his most urgent worry was that his new female body would be sexually abused by men (120).

Schreber's fear of altered bodies, both other people's and his own, is a characteristic discernible in subsequent studies of twentieth-century paranoiacs. Victor Tausk's study of paranoiacs and "the influencing machine" details similar symptoms. Tausk's patients described a machine that exerted mind control through waves or rays characteristically controlling the sexual behavior of the patients. One patient Tausk discussed, a woman named Miss Natalija A., believed she was under the influence of an electrical machine that had replicated her body and the bodies of those close to her. She was the only one who recognized that the manipulation was taking place. Natalija told Tausk that originally the machine had manipulated her sexually through its genitalia, but the machine had subsequently lost its sexual organs, and now "the patient has ceased to experience sexual sensations" (530). Similarly, Hanna Segal, discussing a more recent paranoiac patient, comments that he spoke of "living in a world of duplicates, the duplicates being a combination of him and me, a sort of hybrid figure which he projected everywhere" (26).

Replicated bodies, invasions of bodies, and lone individuals who recognize the transformations are taking place—these elements clearly describe 1950s alien-invasion films. Paranoiac discourse hence provided a framework through which postwar anxieties about altered bodies could find expression. Whereas Schreber's invader was God, and Natalija's was the dehumanizing robot of the early twentieth-century industrial imagination, one key invisible invader of the postwar period has been radiation. Officially, propaganda films that emphasized the potential for nuclear power and downplayed the dangers of radiation were assuaging public fears about radiation. One film of the Bikini Atoll test reassured viewers through images of unharmed animals that had been placed in close proximity to the blast, resulting in *Time Magazine* commenting that "The Thing had grown a little less awful as the result of Bikini" (29). General Groves remarked in 1946 that anyone exposed to radiation "simply took a vacation and in due time became all right again" (qtd. in Szaz 128).[2] Other sources of information, however, were alerting the American public to radiation as the invisible enemy.

David Bradley's *No Place to Hide* (1948) contains the first influential discussion of the dangers of radiation. Bradley, a member of the Radiological Safety Section, which monitored the Bikini test, exposed the "invisible danger from radioactivity" (xxii). Bradley portrays radiation as a dangerous force taken lightly by the Navy soldiers he encounters due to its invisibility. He comments, "the whole business must seem like a very bad dream to the regular Navy men: decks you can't stay on for more than a few minutes but which seem like other decks; air you can't breathe without gas masks but which smells like all other air; water you can't swim in, and good tunas and jacks you can't eat. It's a fouled up world" (104). Because of the invisibility of radiation and the strangeness of the Geiger counters and completely covered "Geiger men," the sailors invested radiation with the quality of the supernatural (104-05). Bradley struggled to concretize the threat of radiation: he told the men that each click on the Geiger counter was equivalent to a small bullet piercing their bodies (110). Nevertheless, as Bradley relates, radiation continued to be associated with "the terrors of the supernatural" (153) by the men, despite his attempts to rationally explain the real dangers associated with radiation contamination.

Bradley's work and other postwar sources indicate that the biggest fear associated with exposure to radiation was loss of manhood. He relates that some of the sailors jokingly expressed their fears: "'that's right,' added another. 'Since I've been out here I've grown seventy years old. I don't care if I don't see another woman. I'm a goner. I'm hopeless'" (111). The commander spoke to Bradley when radiation was discovered in the water coolers and told him that the married soldiers were especially worried (152). Other sources emphasize fear of sexual impotency and sterility being linked with radioactivity. John Hersey's influential account of the victims of Hiroshima emphasizes the effect of radiation on the reproductive systems of those afflicted with radiation sickness (78; 105). The creation of the underclass of hibakusha in Japan to encompass those exposed to radiation blasts effectively resulted in a group of people who were largely barred from marriage and reproduction.[3] In *The Beginning or the End* (1946), Hollywood's first presentation of the atomic bomb, a scene included in a prerelease print shows a ship crew member asking "is it true that if you fool around with this stuff (atomic equipment) long enough, you don't like girls anymore?" (qtd. in Shaneen and Taylor 7-8). Paul Boyer's comprehensive study of postwar discussions of the atomic bomb cites "mass sterility" as a central concern of post-atomic war scenarios. While radiation contamination in reality threatened the body on many levels, the area of concern in the postwar period was male sexuality and reproductive ability.[4]

While radiation threatened to undermine manliness, paradoxically, prolonged exposure to radioactivity became the very measure of manliness. Bradley discerned this paradox in the behavior of the Navy men he encountered. Bradley comments that, "all they [the sailors] wanted from us Geiger men was an assurance of continuing manhood, and they would be willing to tackle an atomic bomb every morning before breakfast, if not before coffee" (25). The Navy crew viewed the Geiger men as "cranky old maids," due to their constant observation of the men's bodies and barracks (124). George B. Kistiakowsky notes the same gendering of those concerned about safety and those boldly risking exposure at Los Alamos, where he worked as chief of the Explosives Division, commenting that Groves viewed the scientists as "effete" (60). Tough soldiers were forced to risk high doses of radiation to prove their manhood at the same time that, in their minds at least, the radiation posed an enormous threat to their sexual and reproductive functions. Paul Boyer relates that the attempt to prove manliness on the part of the Navy commanders resulted in soldiers sleeping in shorts on the decks of contaminated ships (90-91). A rhetorical trap was set whereby those who attempted to decry radiation contamination were labeled feminine and hence suspect men, a method that helped to discredit those who spoke up as "pansies." Sf films of the 1950s, including the three discussed here, frequently associate those who speak out against the invasion—David MacLean, John Putnam, and Miles Bennell—with a marginalized, feminized position.

Bradley's book portrays the invisible enemy of radiation emanating from us, from the very U.S. authority structures that should be protecting citizens. This is a theme relevant to the enemy within, which these sf films are preoccupied with, and is a theme Mumford takes up in his book *In The Name of Sanity*.[5] Mumford fears that the postwar paranoia in the

U.S. will result in Nazi-like experimentation on citizens, leading to "the worst sadism" disguised as "responsible scientific experimentation with live subjects" (30). He foresees a future in which "radioactive water has become the ideal medium of mass extermination" (68): in fact, one plan toyed with at Los Alamos was the use of radioactive food on the Japanese (Dowling 140). Mumford's paranoiac discourse portrays the United States as the evil manipulative power which through radioactive contamination "will ultimately exterminate life in every form" (86). Mumford urges his audience to face the "real" enemy—"an enemy we have yet to confront accusingly in the mirror—ourselves" (109).

Mumford believes that the assertion of humanitarian values is the only way to counter a totalitarian U.S. government bent on poisoning us with radiation: "the restoration of the organic, the human, the personal, to a central place in our economy, is essential if we are to overcome forces that, without such overall-direction and control, are now driving our society ever closer to internal disintegration and external destruction" (60-61). Schreber also asserted his humanity as a defense against the fleeting improvised men, and Tausk's patients emphasized their humanity in the face of the diabolical influencing machines. Humanity is also the rallying cry of the film protagonists David, John, and Miles.

William Cameron Menzies' *Invaders from Mars* (1953), Jack Arnold's *It Came from Outer Space* (1953), and Don Siegel's *Invasion of the Body Snatchers* (1956) all share the paranoiac view of the enemy Other penetrating into the very heart of American 1950s society—the small, suburban town.[6] As if adopting the title of David Bradley's book, the three films tell the postwar audience that there is no place to hide, especially when the small town is located in the American West. Arnold's film sets its action in the Arizona desert; Siegel's locates the drama in Santa Mira, a small California suburb; while the location in Menzies' film is unspecified, it is also a small town, one in close proximity to a military base. Thus the apparently safe environment of the American small town is invaded by a force that either takes over the bodies of its inhabitants (*Invaders*) or produces uncanny replicants of the townspeople (*It Came*), or both (*Invasion*). It is significant that the area in which frequent atomic and hydrogen bomb tests occurred—the American Southwest—serves as an appropriate site for troping the invisible danger of radiation.

In *It Came from Outer Space,* an alien spacecraft is mistaken for a meteor. Interestingly, eyewitness accounts of the explosion at Trinity Site in New Mexico indicate that many of the civilians who witnessed the explosion there believed they had seen a meteor hit the earth (Laurence 195; Szaz 84). In the film, when John, Ellen, and Pete arrive at the crash site, the deep crater is seen to resemble craters left after nuclear bomb tests. Commenting on the supposed meteor, Sheriff Mat Warren says that it "lit up the sky like the end of all creation." His perception of the meteor as apocalyptic strongly resembles descriptions of atomic-bomb explosions. Laurence describes the atomic bomb blast as follows: "it was as though the earth had opened and the skies had split. One felt as though one were present at the moment of creation" (10-11). Similarly, as John and Ellen search for the alien lifeform in the desert, John comments that there are "a thousand ways the desert can kill," and speaks directly to the invader: "I know you're out there hiding in the desert." Later, when the couple meets Frank and George, telephone maintenance workers, Frank comments that "working in the desert you see and hear a lot of things." John has fled the city for the peacefulness of the desert but encounters instead a situation in which an invader forces him to confront the townspeople and himself as radically other, as replicants produced by a mysterious alien presence in the desert.

While *It Came from Outer Space* invokes the literal radiation contamination present at bomb-test locations—radiation that makes the ordinary human other—*Invasion of the Body Snatchers* invokes a paranoiac world in which the very authorities citizens look to for protection from the dangers of radiation are insidiously poisoning them. *Body Snatchers* opens with the titles appearing over rolling clouds. Immediately, the question of whether they are radioactive or natural clouds comes to mind. In Jack Finney's novel, on which the film is based, the alien plant invaders insinuate themselves into Mill Valley (the name of Santa Mira in the novel) by invading clouds and raining into the soil.[7] In Siegel's film, Miles, shocked by Dr. Kauffmann's explanation of the invasion, exclaims, "so that's how it began, out of the sky!" Analogously, one concern at Trinity was that clouds might carry radioactive material many miles away and contaminate areas distant from the test site. However, as Szaz reports, the authorities at Trinity displayed a cavalier attitude toward fallout: "Although the fallout issue eventually proved more important to the nation than atmospheric ignition or the blast wave, discussion of it did not loom large on the scientists' initial list of priorities" (62). Radiation safety existed under the cover of "health physics," and Trinity scientists tested radiation fallout by mailing badges of Eastman Kodak film to various towns in New Mexico, which were returned to the site when they were not picked up (Szaz 122). By 1956, however, public awareness of fallout damage had radically increased due to Bradley's book and to the widely publicized contamination of the Japanese fishing boat *The Lucky Dragon* in 1954, which resulted from an American nuclear test carried out at Bikini Atoll.

When Miles returns to Santa Mira, everything looks the same, but an unseen enemy has invaded the town. The Grimaldi vegetable stand has closed down and Jimmy is running from his transformed mother. The invisible enemy invades the family structure changing Mrs. Grimaldi, Uncle Ira, Mr. Driscoll, and finally Becky herself. Further, the authorities are obfuscating the issue. Dr. Kauffmann attempts to explain the biological changes as psychological ones produced by "worry about what's going on in the world." The replicant body discovered in Jack's basement is unformed, or, perhaps, radiation-burned beyond recognition. This is reminiscent of Hersey's account of Hiroshima in which Father Kleinsorge is reported to have discovered victims "whose faces had been almost blotted out by flash burns" (36). Kleinsorge found humans so changed they appeared to be alien: "He had to keep consciously repeating to himself, 'these are human beings'" (45). In the film, Kauffmann and the policeman reassure Miles and Jack that the body is just a murder victim. When the pods are discovered in Jack's greenhouse, Miles responds, "so much has been discovered in these past few years," as if this kind of unusual occurrence is only to be expected in the postwar world. An enemy that claims the body has invaded Santa Mira, like the small Arizona town in Arnold's film. The authorities, more insidiously than in *It Came,* engage in a misinformation campaign to prevent the truth from emerging.

Rather than focusing on the gradual contamination of the human body by radiation, these three films create a paranoiac world in which what "we" (the U.S.) are doing to our own people is really coming from "them" (aliens from other planets). Mumford, writing his own version of postwar paranoiac discourse, seems to me to indicate the kinds of moves these films make: "since all preparations for mass extermination must be secret, we readily tend to project upon our enemies our own plans for aggression" (*Sanity* 69). Mumford's neat formulation recapitulates Freud's famous formulation in his discussion of Schreber: "what was abolished internally, returns from without" (147). David's situation in *Invaders from Mars* strikingly illustrates this proposition. What David witnesses is hence not a bomb test on the neighboring military base, but an invasion from Mars. Again, clouds presage the arrival of the invaders. The spaceship sinks into the ground after a great illumination, and, as in Arnold's film, it is mistaken for a meteor. This invasion not only allows David to retain faith in authority figures such as Dr. Patricia Blake, Dr. Stuart Kelston, and Col. Fielding, but also allows him to express his anxieties concerning adult judgment through the sinister, transformed parents, who want to contaminate him by forcing him into the sandpit. Like the invaders in Arnold's and Siegel's films, the Martians are hidden and invisible until brought to light by David. However, confronting the aliens in Menzies' film is confronting the monster in the mirror that Mumford invokes. George MacLean's work at the factory is secret. He tells Mary he has had heard "rumors," but cannot elaborate. The transformed George is merely an exaggeration of his earlier self as he slaps David for questioning him about top-secret matters. David has been denied use of Dr. Kelston's telescope because the situation has become "hush-hush." The earth is threatening the whole universe with its atomic rocket. When the military officials discover the mind-control implant device, an electronics expert notes that the U.S. is experimenting with a similar device on white mice. The Martian is acknowledged as being "mankind developed to his utmost intelligence." Further, *Invaders* acknowledges itself as a paranoid dream of postwar America through its ending in which the experience is explained as dream and then invoked as reality as David wakes to the same nightmare. The U.S. caught in a repetition-compulsion of paranoiac displacement is inherent in the narrative structure of Menzies' film.

At the center of *Invaders* is the Martian, which represents humans evolved beyond the need for the body and sexuality, and which, through its asexuality, references postwar anxieties that radiation contamination will result in the loss of sexual difference. *Invaders* bases its Martians on those in H. G. Wells' *War of the Worlds* (1898). In Wells' novel, the Martian invaders are more highly evolved human forms devoid of sexual difference. Wells' narrator comments, "the Martians were absolutely without sex, and therefore without any of the tumultuous emotions that arise from that difference among men" (114). The Martians reproduce asexually in the manner of plants. For Wells, the evolution into a one-sex world relates to fin-de-siècle anxieties about shifting gender norms created most obviously by the New Woman and the Aesthete.[8] For postwar America, while gender norms had first been disrupted by wartime working women and returning traumatized men, perhaps the most dramatic threat to sexual difference was located in radiation contamination and nuclear war.[9] In addition to the literal desexing feared as a result of radiation sickness, postwar journalists predicted the breakdown of gender roles due to the preparation for nuclear war. Joseph and Stewart Alsop, in their dramatically titled article "Your Flesh Should Creep," predict a future in which universal service will result in women and men learning similar "doomsday duties" (49). The very rigidity of gender roles in the ideal 1950s' American home may be seen as an attempt to defend against the desexing feared in connection with radiation and nuclear war. This very desexing is what the three films under discussion here realize.

All three films disrupt heterosexual and gender norms through the activities of alien invaders and position their lone protagonists as humans who fight for "normal" heterosexual relations and reproduction. The Martian spaceship disrupts George and Mary's nighttime activities, and eventually transforms them both into emotionless replicants. When they arrive at the police station to get David, Sgt. Finley says they are "the coldest pair I ever saw." Even David's potential girlfriend, Kathy, is changed into a cold, sexless tool of the Martians. Further, David's surrogate parents, Patricia and Stuart, are largely asexual intellectuals. In the spaceship Patricia is semi-ravished by one of the mutants—her blouse is pulled down over one shoulder—but only so she can receive the implant and become a replicant. In David's flashback before he wakes up, the last image that crosses his mind is his cold, changed mother threatening him in the police station: her transformation is the strongest sign of the disruption of the heterosexual family in the film as she becomes the mother who has lost her nurturing qualities.

Similarly, in *It Came from Outer Space,* the invasion disrupts heterosexual "normality." The ship crashes, thus interfering with John and Ellen's romantic evening, just as she is encouraging him toward marriage. Frank's wife and George's girlfriend testify to the altered men: George's sexy girlfriend even makes a sexual pun about his lack of appetite. Further, as in *Invaders,* the aliens themselves are curiously asexual blobs who ape sexual difference through replicated humans in order to gather the supplies needed to repair their spaceship. Ellen's asexual, emotionless replicant attempts to lure John to his death.

Invasion of the Body Snatchers also portrays the alien invaders as a force that creates an asexual world. Sexuality and sexual difference are *the* measures of humanity in the film. On a date with Becky, Miles kisses her, jokingly commenting, "You're Becky Driscoll." As in *It Came,* the invasion disrupts the possible sexual activity of the heterosexual couple, interfering with Becky and Miles' dates due to the discovery of the body in Jack's basement and the discovery of the pods in Jack's greenhouse. In Finney's novel, Miles states prior to the discovery of the pods: "Then I was kissing her [Becky] again, and suddenly, instantly, I didn't care what happened. I'd never in my life experienced anything like this, and my hand dropped down, tight on her thigh, and I knew I was going to take this girl upstairs with me if I could" (85). However, the changed humans are asexual, promising a world without sexuality and emotion. Human reproduction is replaced by asexual plant reproduction, as Finney's novel makes clear (162). In all three films the transformed woman serves as the site of horror over loss of sexual difference. Thus, as the Mary and Ellen replicants horrify the protagonists with their lack of female warmth, so the transformed Becky frightens Miles. After kissing her replicant, he comments, "I'd been afraid a lot of times in my life, but I didn't know the real meaning of fear until, until I kissed Becky."

One symptomatic feature of paranoia is the assertion on the part of the paranoiac that in an altered world, he or she possesses the "real" humanity and sexual difference needed to save the world. Schreber saw it as his "duty" to "cultivate voluptuousness" which helps effect his transformation into a woman because it will allow for the continuation of the human race (208). Schreber imagined himself as consisting of a male and a female engaged in sexual union (208) in order to assert human sexuality and reproduction in a world of fleeting improvised men. Freud related the paranoiac world to an attempt at recovery after an internal catastrophe: *"the delusion-formation, which we take to be a pathological produce, is in reality an attempt at recovery, a process of reconstruction"* (147). In paranoia, the libido withdraws from the world, focuses on the ego, and then attempts to establish contact with the world again, resulting in the creation of a delusional system. The emphasis on procreation fantasies in paranoia may be related to the desire to repopulate the world that has been perceived as destroyed by catastrophe. Commenting on Schreber, Jacques Lacan observes that Schreber's procreation fantasy "parodies the situation of the couple of ultimate survivors who, following some human catastrophe, would see themselves with the power to repopulate the earth, confronted by the element that the act of animal reproduction bears within itself" (211). When the catastrophe became realizable, as in the postwar period, the paranoiac system became conducive to cultural fantasy rather than just personal fantasy. While early twentieth-century readers could only possibly understand world catastrophe along the lines Schreber hints at, 1950s Americans read on a daily basis the imaging of the end of the world due to atomic war or, more covertly, radiation contamination. Thus the Adam-and-Eve fantasy outlined by Lacan gained new cultural resonance.

Becky and Miles assert their ability to be the lone parents of humans in a world of replicants. After being trapped by the replicants, Miles asserts his love for Becky, and she responds, "I want your children." Yet the dream of the continuation of human sexuality and reproduction is squelched by Becky's transformation. The invisible enemy has altered her into a desexed being. John and Ellen's relationship promises the continuation of human emotion and sexuality, yet both are portrayed as uncanny replicants that threaten the continuation of human reproduction and sexuality. While John's exclamation, "they'll be back," at the end of the film is framed optimistically, the logic of the film suggests that only when humans have evolved into asexual creatures like the aliens themselves—have become all head like the Martian in *Invaders*—will they return. In *Invaders,* David attempts to preserve the human heterosexual family by turning to the new Adam and Eve, Patricia and Stuart, and finally back to the "recovered" George and Mary, yet the film's structure suggests that the nightmare of transformation into an asexual Other never ends.[10]

While the specter of radiation contamination and its disruption of humanity, gender, and sexuality is raised in these three films, the threat is ultimately bound in different ways in them. In my opinion, *Invasion* most powerfully registers the fear by arguing that there is no transformation back from being a replicant. The contaminated body cannot be cured by a vacation. Siegel's original ending, which closes the film after Miles screams, "You're next!" into the camera, registers an intense fear, expressed through a paranoiac world vision, of radiation contamination. Siegel's alternative titles to the film, *Sleep No More* and *Better Off Dead,* register anxiety about radiation contamination as much as they register anxiety about communism.[11] Bradley comments repeatedly on a sleeping American public that is allowing radiation contamination to continue: "how like America, where only the very few know what is really going on behind the darkness and barbed wire," and what effects experimentation will have on human lives (142). Bradley emphasizes that the ignorance of the American public poses the greatest danger to the future: he views an ill-informed American public as more threatening than a well-informed foreign power (165). *Invasion of the Body Snatchers* allegorizes an America that is being poisoned and transformed in its sleep in the safety of suburbia.

By contrast, *Invaders* and *It Came* both suggest that transformation is only temporary. George and Mary are made other, but are saved by an operation that removes the mind-control device. Further, in the film the very force that threatens contamination (the military) saves humanity. The film reassures by suggesting that the enemy is really the savior, exhibiting a typical feature of paranoiac discourse in which denial-projective displacement soothes the paranoiac. Thus instead of concluding it is them (the military) who are poisoning us, the film concludes that is them (the Martians) who are changing us, but it is them (the military) who are saving us.[12]

It Came from Outer Space goes ever further in reassuring the audience about the transformed bodies. Because the aliens are peaceful, they merely replicate the human to escape the hostilities of earth. The aliens reassure John that they do not wish to take souls, minds, or bodies from the earth people. While some critics have commented on the progressive politics of the film, from my perspective, the film defuses the threat of radiation contamination it raises by suggesting that not only can the humans be restored to normality, but that they haven't really been changed at all.[13] Unlike *Invasion* and *Invaders, It Came* achieves diegetic closure with the heterosexual couple reunited and faith restored in the safety of everyday life. As John and Ellen look up to the sky, it is no longer a source of danger, but presages the further evolution of humans into creatures like the aliens.

Because nuclear war and widespread radiation contamination have never occurred, they must necessarily exist in the realm of fantasy. What I have been arguing is that 1950s sf films tap into the paranoiac fantasy of a postwar American public faced not only with the fable of apocalyptic nuclear war, but with the fable of something more insidious—invisible radiation contamination. Like the paranoiac, these films attempt to reconstruct the world after catastrophe, but also like the paranoiac, as Lacan remarks, "the problem lies not in the reality that is lost, but that which takes its place" (188-89). These paranoiac visions make the slow battle with radiation-produced cancer into fabulous stories of lone humans battling a world of alien others. At the same time, like paranoiac delusion, these films decry a national security state that is insecure, and that, as we know 50 years later, did conduct radiation experiments on its citizens.[14] In their attempts to make manifest the invisible invader, these films provide glimpses into anxieties of postwar America.[15]

Further ways in which nuclear anxiety impacted the domestic and gender roles constitute the focus of the following three chapters of the book. In 1950s sf films the nuclear threat frequently invades the haven of the middle-class home. Thus the very image of safety in the postwar world—the nuclear family and its shelter—becomes the most dangerous of locations. Similarly, the supposed bedrock of the postwar separate spheres is called into question by the effects of the atomic bomb. Masculinity, femininity, domesticity, and the body itself become radically destabilized in these sf fantasies. I begin with a discussion of the particular symptomology of feminine paranoia in the postwar era.

4

FEMININE PARANOIA AND SECRECY:
I MARRIED A MONSTER FROM OUTER SPACE
AND *ATTACK OF THE 50 FT. WOMAN*

The 1950s security state was one in which knowledge and ignorance were often demarcated along gender lines. Middle-class women, and especially housewives, were sheltered, at least ideally, from the harsh realities of the specter of nuclear war, the Cold War, and the espionage scenarios that troubled postwar American society. Recent commentators on the Rosenberg Trial, for example, have argued that Ethel Rosenberg's demonization in the press resulted from an American public indignant about a woman who renounced her roles as wife and mother to become a rigid ideologue.[1] As Robert Meeropol, son of Julius and Ethel, argues, although privately government agents believed Julius "was the dominant political force in the family," publicly, Ethel bore the brunt of their act of espionage through the American people's perception of her as a cold, unnatural woman (242). Reflecting on the Rosenberg Trial raises issues about the American public's belief in secrecy and in a clear line between the safe domestic haven and the dangerous Atomic Age. As I argue, the emphasis on the preservation of feminine innocence in a dangerous post-World-War-II world fostered a feminine paranoiac vision. This chapter traces this feminine cultural paranoia through the historical reality of Los Alamos and through two 1950s sf films, *I Married a Monster from Outer Space* and *Attack of the 50 Ft. Woman,* films that express fears about postwar society through feminine paranoiac scenarios.

Personal accounts by the women who lived and worked at Los Alamos reveal a world in which scientist husbands were engaged in mysterious work that fostered the suspicions of wives. The official policy at Los Alamos was that, due to the perceived security risks involved, wives could be informed neither of the purpose of the project nor of the nature of the individual work done by their husbands. What the personal accounts of these women reveal is that this denial of knowledge created a situation in which paranoiac fantasies filled the gap occasioned by the secret reality. In Laura Fermi's account of her marriage to physicist Enrico Fermi, she relates how secrecy concerning his work

51

resulted in her being forced to trust a faceless "they": discussing their impending move to Chicago, she states: "Enrico was unhappy to move. *They* (I did not know who they were) had decided to concentrate all *that* work (I did not know what it was) in Chicago, and enlarge it greatly, Enrico grumbled" (169). After Enrico set off the first controlled-nuclear-fission reaction in December 1942, a key occurrence leading toward the construction of the atomic bomb, Laura was perplexed by the congratulations showered upon him. She asked two of Enrico's colleagues what he had accomplished, and they told her he had sunk a Japanese admiral. Perplexed, Laura thought to herself: "They should know. To sink a ship in the Pacific from Chicago . . . perhaps power rays were discovered . . ." (179). Due to her inability to know what Enrico was working on, she was forced to construct fantasies that filled in the gap of her ignorance.

Other women at Los Alamos made similar comments about their experiences there. Elsie McMillan, wife of physicist Edwin McMillan, discussed the relief she felt when another scientist's wife told her that the men were working on an atomic bomb.[2] Elsie wrote that "One night I said to my husband, 'Why didn't you tell me you're making an atomic bomb?' He said, 'My god, where did you hear that? Do you know you could get me fired?' I replied, 'Somebody told me but I'm not going to tell you who it was'" (42). Elsie stated that she felt relief as a result of this knowledge "because I could better understand when my husband left me for places unknown, when he worked all hours of the day and night, when he looked so drawn, tired, worried" (42). Those wives not informed were forced to feel a vague, undefined fear. Bernice Brode, wife of physicist Robert Brode, expressed the vague fear she experienced: "Even an outsider like myself, with no idea what the problem was, could feel the inner urge for scientific solution" (146).[3]

Eleanor Jette's account of her life at Los Alamos with metallurgist husband, Eric, highlights how the issues of secrecy versus knowledge were played out in the domestic realm of the secret city. Before their departure for Los Alamos, Eleanor, who had previously had some training in chemistry and physics, attempted to discern the truth of the secret project. As she searched through chemistry journals for references to uranium or thorium, Eric scrutinized her (12). Attempting to discuss the project with Eric, Eleanor was rebuffed (12). When Eleanor began to speculate that a nuclear weapon was being built, Eric became horrified by her guesswork. Angry at the living conditions at Los Alamos, Eleanor exclaimed, "He [Oppenheimer] can get someone else to work on his new fangled super bomb" (56-57). Eric reacted with terror: "Oh my God! Where did you get that idea?" (57). Because Eleanor could not discuss the project, she created a paranoiac vision in which "Los Alamos was like a giant anthill. The atom bomb was its queen and the Tech area was her nest. The Queen's demands for nourishment were unceasing" (42).[4] While Eleanor had to construct fantasies to account for the realities of the work at the laboratory, the effects on her daily life were real. Her cat, Mikey, for example, died of radiation poisoning, and she had to speculate privately how this had occurred: "Mikey, somehow, some way, had gotten a dose of the deadly stuff they used in the Tech Area into her system. Whether it was by hunting in a contaminated area . . . I neither knew, nor cared. I was heartsick" (88). Los Alamos wives were forced to create delusions to explain the frightening and mysterious realities of their everyday lives.

The accounts of Jette and others point out that the secrecy maintained in Los Alamos homes resulted in domestic strife and created suspicion of the husbands on the part of the wives. Eleanor's marriage to Eric became strained soon after their arrival at Los Alamos: "Eric doesn't say anything . . . I hope he isn't going to do the strong, silent act indefinitely" (27). Eric asked Eleanor to leave the room during several conversations with colleagues, and this resulted in Eleanor angrily waiting in the bedroom (29). Commenting on the Los Alamos wives in general, Eleanor stated, "We occupied the sidelines of history and our role was not easy. It was up to us to see that our men were fed and loved and kept serene, so they could give their full attention to the Bomb . . . We coped with our problems alone" (45-46). Eleanor Stone Roensch, a WAC at Los Alamos, also gave an account of the strain put on domestic life at Los Alamos and the nightmares produced by vague rumors "about this mysterious weapon" (39). L. D. P. King, a physicist at Los Alamos, noted that Oppenheimer was plagued with complaints from Los Alamos wives: "he also had to soothe some of the irate scientists' wives for all sorts of domestic problems and failings in the townsite" (66).

The atmosphere of secrecy that pervaded wartime Los Alamos and probably the entire U.S. postwar security state fostered feminine paranoia on the part of women denied knowledge of nuclear weapons, yet uncomfortably living with the fear and anxiety experienced by their husbands.[5] Sociological studies of paranoia in the United States have concluded that a prime factor influencing the development of paranoiac symptoms is powerlessness.[6] When the war ended, American middle-class people in general began to be encouraged to concoct scenarios analogous to those concocted by the Los Alamos wives. Thus, in a 1946 article, Harold C. Urey, a Los Alamos scientist, frightens his readers: "My point is this: a few years from now, that fear may come home to you. By that time you will no longer feel so relaxed and carefree—happy that the war is over. A few years from now you may be wondering what is going on behind the locked doors of laboratories all over the world, just as we once wondered, night and day" (18).[7]

Indeed, in the postwar period, a deep sense of powerlessness began to infect women and some other groups, and this sense resulted in the spread among women of a general suspicion and fear of nuclear power, and particularly of nuclear weapons: Spencer Weart notes that gender has been the area of decisive split regarding perceptions of nuclear power: "a strong divergence turned up in every poll, in every country, at every time . . . twice as many women as men spoke anxiously about dangers" (367). In a 1995 Gallup poll 61 percent of the men polled and 29 percent of the women polled said they would have ordered the bomb to be dropped in 1945 (qtd. in Lifton and Mitchell 303n). On the individual level, feminine paranoia resulting from secrecy most frequently centered on the husband: intimate partner or monster? 1950s sf asked. Before examining the two sf films under discussion here, I want to implicate the postwar security state with psychoanalytic theories of paranoia in order to examine how a particular type of feminine paranoia emerges in representations of the 1950s housewife.

One characteristic of paranoiac thinking is that the initial suspicion, which will eventually result in the creation of a delusional system, first centers on a loved one, usually the spouse. In Daniel Paul Schreber's classic text of paranoiac thinking, his suspicion falls on those close to him, his physicians and his wife. Looking out the asylum window at his wife, Schreber concluded that she was no longer a human but one of the "fleeting-improvised" humans whom he believed to people the world (68). Norman Cameron notes that most involved paranoiac delusions begin "with personal matters" and are most often centered on those with whom the paranoiac is sexually intimate ("Pseudo-Community" 36). While the transformation of a loved one into a monster to be feared is typical of many paranoiac scenarios, feminine paranoiac transformation has a particular symptomology.

Using a Freudian model, I want to suggest that women because of their psychic development are particularly susceptible to paranoia regarding their sexual partners. In Lecture XXXIII of *New Introductory Lectures on Psychoanalysis,* Freud links the pre-oedipal infant's fear of the mother to the beginnings of paranoiac thinking: "thus, for instance, one discovers the fear of being murdered or poisoned, which may later on form the nucleus of a paranoiac disorder, already present in this pre-oedipal stage and directed against the mother" (164). Freud goes on to discuss the particular difficulty of the formation of the female subject. Unlike the male subject, who transfers his desire for the mother to a more acceptable object of the female sex, the female subject must negotiate more difficult terrain: "this step in development is not merely a question of a change of object. The turning away from the mother occurs in an atmosphere of antagonism; the attachment to the mother ends in hate" (165). The terms Freud uses here to describe the development of the "normal" feminine psyche sound much like his description of paranoiac thinking in his commentary on Schreber. Thus, discussing Schreber's descent into paranoia, Freud argues that the basis of the transformation relies upon an initial thought: "*I* (a man) *love him* (a man)" (139). Because this thought was unacceptable to Schreber, and is so to paranoiacs in general, the thought becomes transformed into: "I do not love him—I *hate* him" (139), and this new thought becomes in turn transformed by projection into: "He *hates* (persecutes) *me,* which will justify me in hating him" (139). The final acceptable transformation, this time into an acceptable thought, is: "I do not *love* him—I *hate* him because HE PERSECUTES ME" (139). While, in his discussion of Schreber, Freud is interested in theorizing paranoia as a defense against homosexuality, the following transformation would appear to characterize the "normal" course of feminine psychic development: "I (a woman) love her (my mother)" must become: "I do not love her (my mother)—I hate her because she (the pre-oedipal mother) persecutes me." In Lecture XXXIII Freud observes that women remain in this paranoiac relationship with the mother for "an indefinite period," abandoning it "late in life, and then incompletely" (177). Thus "normal" feminine psychic development seems to be development in which the female subject lives out a paranoiac delusion in relation to the pre-oedipal mother.

How does the husband become the object of feminine paranoiac delusion? In Lecture XXXIII Freud suggests that the female subject's husband, who originally appeared to be receiving the desire transferred from the father to him, "comes in the course of time to inherit the position of the mother as well" (182). For the female subject, all intimate relationships ultimately are unconsciously with the mother and, due to her vexed development into a heterosexual subject, they are also paranoiac ones. Freud comments: "In this way it may easily occur that the second part of a woman's life is taken up with a struggle against her husband, just as the shorter earlier part was occupied with rebellion against her mother" (182).

In "A Case of Paranoia Running Counter to the Psycho-Analytic Theory of the Disease," Freud analyzes a female paranoiac whose case appears to follow such a course as is outlined above. This woman has delusions of being photographed while she is having sexual relations with her lover. While manifestly her delusions and anger are directed at her lover, Freud speculates "that the persecutor is at bottom someone whom the patient loves or has loved in the past" (265). As her delusions develop, an elderly female supervisor at her job emerges as a persecutor as well. The woman patient suspects that her lover and the supervisor are plotting against her (268). In transferring her desire to an appropriate heterosexual mate, the female subject risks experiencing all intimate relationships from a paranoiac position. Although Freud uses this case study to argue for paranoia as a psychic defense against homosexual desire, the terms he uses in the analysis would apply to all female subjects: "as a rule we find that the victim of persecution remains fixated to the same persons, and therefore to the same sex to which his love-objects belonged before the paranoiac transformation took place" (271).

According to Freud's description of the feminine psyche, the original love object of all women was the pre-oedipal mother: thus, she will be the persecutor behind the husband. Following Freud's schema, it is also possible to state that heterosexual attachments for women are paranoiac, because they are the result of a warding off of same-sex desire for the mother. Thus paranoia is not a homosexual psychosis but a heterosexual one: those who defend against homosexual desire *are* heterosexual subjects in the Freudian world.[8] For heterosexual women, because of the difficult transference of desire, paranoia seems more likely to center on the figure behind whom looms the pre-oedipal mother—the husband. In a postwar age of heightened cultural paranoiac delusions that intersected with private psychic conflicts, for the 1950s housewife, the domestic realm could be as much a world of suspicion and conspiracy as the outside world could be for her husband.

Viewed within this context, Gene Fowler's *I Married a Monster from Outer Space* (1958) may be seen as a feminine analogue of Don Siegel's *Invasion of the Body Snatchers* (1956), a postwar nightmare of changed identities seen from the perspective of a 1950s housewife. On one level, the film illustrates the difficulties of a young woman entering sexual maturity. Marge, the protagonist, must transfer her affection from her mother to her new husband. In an uncanny version of adult sexuality, Marge marries an alien who has used Bill's body to disguise himself on earth. At their wedding, Marge's mother is portrayed as tormenting her because Bill is late. When the alien Bill arrives, he kisses Marge intently, prompting Marge's mother to comment, "Marge, you're not married yet!" Marge's virginity, which is referenced in this comment, while making her the ideal 1950s good girl, also makes her vulnerable. Unable to recognize "normal" heterosexual behavior, she accepts the alien Bill as a typical husband. When Bill and Marge arrive at their honeymoon hotel, she tells him, "I've never been on a honeymoon before." He responds, "Neither have I." Marge accepts Bill's virginity as the explanation for his strange behavior.

After a year of marriage, Marge still feels her attachment to her mother unchanged: she is unable to transfer her desire to Bill. We see Marge writing a letter to her mother: "Maybe it's me, but, oh, Mama, Bill isn't the man I fell in love with." She crumples-up the letter, indicating that it is a fantasy mother, or maternal imago, to whom she is writing. Because the film operates within the logic of feminine paranoiac delusion, it affirms her suspicion of Bill as alien, rather than portraying it as a delusion that shelters Marge from the difficult course to heterosexual womanhood. One characteristic of paranoiac delusion centering on a sexual partner is that the sexual partner is controlling the paranoiac's sexuality: internal desire becomes displaced to external manipulation. R. V. Krafft-Ebing discusses a female paranoiac who believed her seducer "impelled her to sexual acts" (495). Victor Tausk's study of "the influencing machine" documents paranoiacs who feel their sexuality is controlled by external machines. One woman discussed by Tausk believed that when her machine double had its genitalia manipulated, she herself became sexually aroused (535). This belief in external control replacing internal desire is relevant for Marge: her paranoiac vision results in her desire being projected onto the alien she has married, an alien who has taken her virginity and who ultimately wants to reproduce his race through her human body.[9]

In an interesting discussion of paranoia that is relevant for *I Married a Monster from Outer Space,* Harry Stack Sullivan discusses paranoiac delusion in terms of the uncanny. In Sullivan's view, the projection that occurs in paranoia is a projection of the internal "not-me," the internal other, onto an external source: "as a result, that which was dissociated, and which was in a certain meaningful sense related to the not-me, is now definitely *personified* as not-me, that is, as *others.* And the others carry the blame of that which had previously had to be maintained in dissociation as an intolerable aspect of one's own personal possibilities" (361). In his commentary on Sullivan's theory, Russell Meares theorizes that it is intimacy with another person which brings about the split between me and not-me, resulting in the projection of the unacceptable not-me onto an external source: "the fragile conception of self boundary leaves the individual vulnerable as intimacy develops. Experiences of disintegration may come about through such traumata as separation from a self-object, intrusion into core experience, and negative responses to self-revelation. Among the consequences of this disintegration are paranoid ideas" (664). Implicating these theories of paranoia with Freud's schema of feminine psychic development, I suggest that the not-me within the female subject may be the pre-oedipal mother, whom the woman once loved, but has had to learn to hate, and then to transform her hatred into paranoiac delusions of persecution. For Marge, the uncanny not-me mother emerges in her first heterosexual partner, Bill. She is saved from identification with the feared mother by projecting her onto Bill, the monster she has unwittingly married.

The fact that Fowler's film frames itself as a feminine paranoiac delusion becomes clear in its early scenes.[10] Bill's bachelor party is every bride-to-be's nightmare. Bill and his friends drink heavily, exchanging cynical comments about marriage. One friend states, "Seeing her [the bride] at the wedding, that's bad luck." One man suggests mass suicide as a solution to marriage. Bill is portrayed as superior to his friends when he leaves early intending to check on Marge; however, he is stopped on the road by a double of his body, which causes him to be abducted by aliens.

The film constructs a pseudo-community of evil men who threaten and persecute women. The film creates two pseudo-communities of threatening men: on the one hand, Bill's cynical friends, who regard marriage as a prison; on the other hand, the aliens, which take over male human bodies exclusively in order to use female humans to repopulate their race. Good men like Bill and his friend Sam, who do not look upon marriage unfavorably, are susceptible to alien take-over for that very reason—because they are willing to marry and thus provide the aliens with women with whom to reproduce.

Like a typical paranoiac scenario, *I Married a Monster from Outer Space* emphasizes the moment of clarity when Marge realizes that all her suspicions are justified. In an early article on paranoia, "Further Remarks on the Neuro-Psychoses of Defence" (1896), Freud outlines this moment of clarification as central to paranoia. Discussing a female paranoiac, Freud writes, "She spoke of a certain moment in her illness at which for the first time 'everything became clear to her'—that is, at which she became convinced of the truth of her suspicion" (177). Cameron discusses the moment of clarification as the "final delusional reconstruction of reality" in which the paranoiac exclaims, "I suddenly realized what it was all about!" ("Revisited" 56). Sullivan views this clarification as the sign that the paranoiac "has started living in a world in which not-me has become personified, very active, and very absorptive of one's weakness" (362). In the film, Marge follows Bill into the woods where her suspicions about his otherness are confirmed. Bill's alien self emerges from the human shell it has appropriated and walks into the spaceship, and Marge realizes that what she has taken to be Bill is in fact a puppet, which is animated by the alien inside the shell.

Marge's realization that her husband is an alien is further compounded by the gradual revelation the film makes that a pseudo-community of male authority figures has been taken over by the aliens, and when this aspect of the film is examined, Marge's status as powerless 1950s housewife living in a world of secrecy and fear comes out strongly. The invasion of the secure domestic world by a dangerous, uncanny Atomic Age is revealed. Bill, ostensibly an insurance salesman, brings Marge anything but safety. For help, she turns to Chief Collins of the police force, who is not only a representative of the law, but also her godfather. Collins attempts to discount her belief in the spaceship by getting her to believe it to be a cultural delusion: he tells her that there have been many reports about landings; however, like Bill, Collins himself has already been abducted, and she is, in fact, speaking to *his* alien double, which goes on to threaten her with an asylum when she persists with her investigation, the asylum being the "appropriate" place for the powerless, curious postwar woman. Other policemen also turn out to be members of the pseudo-community: in one scene they vaporize a "useless" drunk who has witnessed Marge's fear after the moment of clarification and asks too many questions about that fear. The aliens take over the town's communications channels. Marge attempts to contact Washington, D.C., but is prevented from doing so by the operator. She attempts to send a telegram to the FBI, but it is destroyed. She tries to leave town, but the roads are blocked. All these scenes emphasize her powerlessness. Afterwards, she asks the alien substitute for Bill, "Does frightening women make you proud?" Because paranoiac visions protect the ego from confrontation with powerlessness, Marge is protected from the realization that in the postwar period the degree of a housewife's ignorance and lack of social power measure her appeal in the "safe" domestic haven. The 1950s housewife was to supply a comfortable resort for her husband, a well-ordered home that offered him refuge from the stresses of the outside world. David Halberstam comments that the 1950s woman "devotedly raised her family, supported her husband, kept her house spotless and efficient, got dinner ready on time, and remained attractive and optimistic" (590). Curiosity and fear were clearly not part of this ideal vision of femininity. In Marge's world, however, these qualities are necessary so that the domestic realm can be saved.

As is typical in paranoiac scenarios, Marge eventually saves the human race from destruction. Thus, for example, just as Schreber believed he had to be transformed into a woman in order to repopulate a destroyed human race, Marge saves the human race from evolutionary take-over by the aliens, which, once they have abducted human men, intend to reduce their own race through the use of human women.

Marge is able to save humans through the help of a pseudo-community of friends, real humans who believe her and band together. Cameron notes that a pseudo-community of friends ("Revisited" 56) frequently complements the pseudo-community of enemies in paranoiac delusion. Marge finds her friends in Dr. Wayne, an obstetrician whom she has visited earlier to discuss why she and the pseudo-Bill cannot have children, and in all the men in her community who have recently become fathers. The ability to reproduce becomes the measure of human men. Thus while the alien men bespeak the difficulties of both feminine psychical development and postwar secrecy, Marge's friends reaffirm heterosexual reproductive normality. Marge saves the human race and is reunited with the real Bill at the end of the film.

Nathan Juran's *Attack of the 50 Ft. Woman* (1958) also implicates a feminine paranoiac vision with postwar anxieties. Like Fowler's film, Juran's film focuses on a troubled marriage, but whereas the aliens in *I Married* are postulated as the cause of Bill and Marge's bad marriage, the aliens in *Attack* provide a brief respite for Nancy Fowler Archer in her disastrous marriage to her philandering, gold-digging husband, Harry Archer. Dr. Cushing attributes Nancy's alcoholism, violent headaches, and incarcerations in asylums to her bad marriage. Cushing speculates that after her marriage, Nancy has allowed her emotions to control her health. Von Loeb, a specialist called in after Nancy becomes fifty-foot tall, comments that her unhappy marriage is "a case not infrequent in this supersonic age we live in." Even though Cushing and Von Loeb are presented with empirical proof of Nancy's transformation, they still seek psychological causes for her change, causes linked to a postwar world of fear and secrecy.

Paradoxically, the very sources of postwar anxiety are put forth by the film as providing Nancy with the means of achieving revenge on her husband. The film opens with scenes of the California desert. For 1950s Americans, the Western desert indicated atmospheric bomb tests and the specter of radiation.[11] This opening sequence is followed by a news report which serves to conflate UFO sightings and uneasiness about nuclear weapons. Nancy's anger at her husband's affair with Honey drives her to the potentially radioactive desert. Here she encounters a spaceship and a giant. When she convinces Harry to go back to the desert with her later, he leaves her to the giant alien. Instead of killing Nancy, however, the alien contaminates her with radiation and makes her into a powerful fifty-foot giant. Cushing finds radiation in the scratch on Nancy's throat inflicted on her by the giant.

In a typical paranoiac move, Nancy believes the aliens have chosen her for some purpose. Similarly, in Schreber's account of his paranoiac delusions, he emphasizes his belief that he is a chosen figure with purpose. Schreber comments that his situation is a chosen one because he has been designated to fight for the good of the human race (130). Nancy also feels that she had this kind of chosen status: she tells Harry that she thinks the ship is waiting for her in the desert. The alien ship does seek her out because of her diamond necklace, which is needed to power the ship, but also it grants her a chance to get revenge. It gives her superhuman status in much the same way that Schreber believed that the rays of God were allowing him to rejuvenate the human race and to survive the destruction of his internal organs.

The aliens give Nancy a mixed gift: superhuman strength, size, and uniqueness, qualities, which, however, make her vulnerable to ridicule. As Nancy watches a newscast after her first sighting of the spaceship, the newscaster taunts her. He says that perhaps the giant is "a man who could love her for herself." He comments on her money and her unsuccessful marriage. Delusions of taunting in the media appear in many instances of paranoia. Schreber recounts that he has read his own obituary in a newspaper, an incident which alerted him to the fact that he could no longer hope to return to normal human society (91). Sandor Ferenczi describes a female paranoiac who suffered from delusions of jealousy regarding her husband, and who was convinced that "between the lines of the local newspaper were innumerable insinuations of her supposed moral depravity and of her ridiculous position as a betrayed wife; the articles were written by journalists at the orders of her enemies" (165). Nancy's enemies, the aliens, allow her to be ridiculed in the press, by her husband, and by everyone in the town, but they also allow her to be affirmed as right. The whole town has to accept her sighting as real and Harry has to accept her anger at his infidelities as literally enormous.

Nancy's transformation into the Other points to a fundamental difference in the ways *I Married* and *Attack* approach the issue of feminine paranoia. Whereas Marge's vision makes her husband into a monster behind whom the pre-oedipal mother is lurking, Nancy's vision relies upon identification with and transformation into the powerful, frightening pre-oedipal maternal imago. In "Mourning and Melancholia," Freud discusses the melancholic person in a manner suggestive for examining both feminine psychic development and feminine paranoia. Freud argues that melancholia is characterized by a loss that remains mysterious to the person because it is a loss that is unconscious in contrast with the loss present in mourning, which is conscious. Freud describes the melancholic person as withdrawing his or her libido from the world and then withdrawing the libido into the ego. In Freud's view, these withdrawals lead to the establishment of "an *identification* of the ego with the abandoned object" (249). Freud sees this identification as "a regression from one type of object-choice to original narcissism" (249). Freud's account here is suggestive for two reasons. First, this account of the development of melancholia bears striking resemblances to his discussion of the first stages of paranoia. Discussing Schreber, Freud traces the process of paranoia beginning with a withdrawal of libido from the world and fixation of libido to the ego which is used "for the aggrandizement of the ego," indicating a return "to the stage of narcissism" ("Psychoanalytic Notes" 148). The final stage in paranoia is the delusional world produced by the desire to recover and reconstruct reality ("Psychoanalytic Notes" 147). Melancholia and paranoia would seem to traverse similar psychic paths with the exception that identification characterizes melancholia and delusion characterizes paranoia.

Second, in terms of the relationship between feminine psychic development and paranoia, "Mourning and Melancholia" provides useful theoretical possibilities. For the female subject, the obscure lost object, which was once loved, but then lost through hatred and then paranoiac fear, is the pre-oedipal mother. Melancholia provides a means of identification with this lost object, but a means that fosters the presence of paranoiac tendencies already implicit in feminine psychic development. Melancholia relies upon a conflict between love and hate for the lost object, which is reminiscent of Freud's discussion of the female subject's struggle with the maternal imago: "in melancholia, accordingly, countless separate struggles are carried on over the object, in which hate and love contend with each other; the one seeks to detach the libido from the object, the other to maintain this position of the libido against the assault" ("Melancholia" 256). Thus the feminine psyche is vulnerable to melancholic identification with the pre-oedipal mother as well as paranoiac fear of her.

Nancy Archer travels the path of identification. Whereas Marge dispels the not-me maternal imago by projecting it onto Bill as alien, Nancy suffers from melancholia, as her depression, alcoholism, and self-hatred indicate. In the paranoiac vision of the film, however, the aliens provide the means for Nancy literally to become the frightening, powerful pre-oedipal mother with whom she has been ambivalently identifying. While Nancy, like Marge, has to fear a dangerous mother disguised as a husband, Nancy defeats the mother by becoming her, and when Harry goes into Nancy's bedroom to murder her, she has grown huge and frightens him away.

Nancy's transformation allows her to become the powerful pre-oedipal mother as, dressed Amazon-like, she tramps through the desert toward the place where she will murder Harry. For 1950s Americans, however, she is a complex image of frightening matriarchal power and atomic mutation.[12] Her anger is the anger of a woman betrayed by her husband and also the anger of an age afraid of the dangers lurking in the radioactive desert, dangers which could radically transform the human body. As Nancy walks through the desert, she passes a drunken prospector who curses the popularity of uranium mines. Nancy's transformation ultimately results in her own destruction as well as Harry's and Honey's —her complete fusion with pre-oedipal mother can consummate itself only in death, just as her radioactive body must be destroyed since it stands as a frightening reminder of the dangers of radiation.

War and postwar feminine paranoia find complex expression in the accounts of the Los Alamos women, who first experienced the secrecy of the Cold War, which divided husband from wife, and also in these two 1950s sf films with their representations of the housewife and her paranoiac scenarios. *I Married a Monster from Outer Space* and *Attack of the 50 Ft. Woman* are unique within a body of sf paranoiac films of the 1950s in presenting the paranoia that begins in the domestic realm. The masculine analogues of these two films, *Invasion of the Body Snatchers* (1956) and Bert Gordon's *The Amazing Colossal Man* (1957) begin with the paranoiac transformation occurring in the professional world of men. In an age of widespread cultural paranoia, these accounts of the specifics of feminine paranoia highlight the difficulties of living in a domestic world supposedly sheltered from postwar realities, but actually teeming with the paranoia of the Atomic Age.

The gendering of the Atomic Age has dimensions beyond men and women. The world of the paranoiac is one that is rigidly gendered. In Schreber's delusional system, for example, the whole animate and inanimate world takes on gender. Schreber relates that beds, hand-mirrors, rakes, and draughts are feminine; basket chairs, spades, and chess are masculine (141-42). Since the paranoiac frequently suffers from the question what sex am I? the entire world must become gendered to help clarify sexual difference. 1950s cultural paranoia also sought to gender and sexualize the Atomic Age, but did so in many paradoxical ways. While nuclear weapons were masculinized through their phallic shape, they were also associated with a primal female power. The following two chapters explore the gendering and sexualization of the Atomic Age as represented in sf films.

Dr. J. Robert Oppenheimer, atomic physicist and head of the Manhattan Project.
Ca. 1944. Courtesy of the National Archives.

Aerial view of Nagasaki, Japan, after atomic bombing in 1945. Courtesy of the Library of Congress.

"Trinity" explosion at Alamagordo, NM, 7/16/45. Courtesy of the National Archives.

Atomic cloud during Baker Day blast at Bikini, 1946. Courtesy of the National Archives.

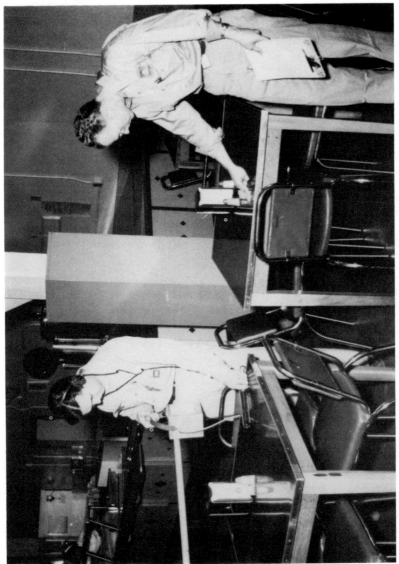

Geiger Men. Courtesy of the Department of Energy.

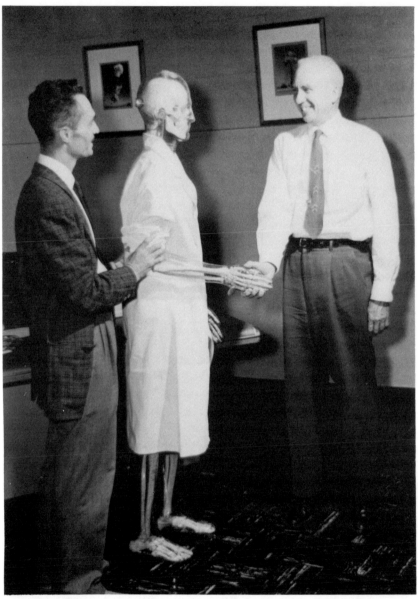

Wright Lanham (left) introduces the "plastic man" to Los Alamos director Norris Bradbury. The figure was used to simulate human radiation exposures. Courtesy of the Department of Energy.

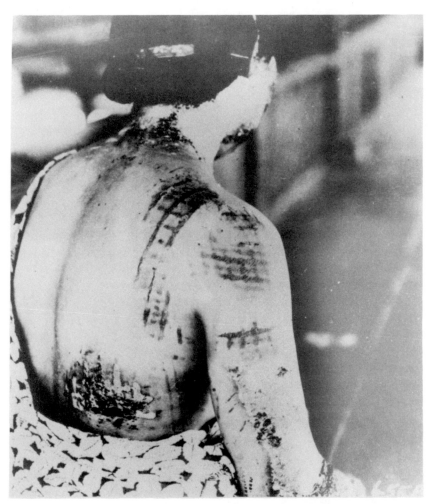

Japanese victim of atomic bombing, 1945. Courtesy of the National Archives.

The anti-Communist (in)security state, 1948. Artist: Bill Mauldin. Courtesy of the Library of Congress.

Nuclear reactor sitting on a test cell pad prior to preliminary tests at the Nevada Test Site (ca. 1968). This Phoebus 2 design was part of the Rover Project to develop a nuclear-propelled rocket for interplanetary travel. Courtesy of the Department of Energy.

Nevada Test Site. Members of the party of 17 Canadian and UK observers at the 400-foot tower shot at Frenchman Flat are shown illuminated by both the sun and the blast. Courtesy of the National Archives.

5

DARWIN AND THE ATOM:
EVOLUTION/DEVOLUTION FANTASIES
IN *THE BEAST FROM 20,000 FATHOMS, THEM!*
AND *THE INCREDIBLE SHRINKING MAN*

The Atomic Age offered a double-edged sword to the American public. Atomic energy was portrayed as the force that could lead postwar society to a utopian existence; the atomic bomb threatened to plunge the world into a horrific dystopia. In a 1946 pamphlet entitled *The Atomic Age: Suicide . . . Slavery or Social Planning?* Aaron Levenstein characterized this two-fold perception of the age: "For the first time in man's long journey out of the dark cave in which he started, the bright sun awaits him. It will not take much now to send him scurrying back to the cave" (29). Levenstein's reference frames the Atomic Age within an evolution/devolution context. In this view, the postwar world has the potential to ascend to Platonic heights of wisdom or to hurl itself back into a caveman-like existence. The Darwinian opposition between evolving and devolving which postwar America inherited from Victorian social theory is an opposition which partakes of the simple logic of paranoia.[1] 1950s B-sf films create paranoiac worlds in which the thin line between ascending to new human heights and falling to animalistic lows are imaginatively broached. This chapter focuses on three classic sf films—*The Beast from 20,000 Fathoms, Them!*, and *The Incredible Shrinking Man*—which examine the potential eclipsing of the human species brought about by the atomic bomb and its psychological and physiological effects in the postwar era.

In popular publications of the late 1940s, the use of the atomic bomb on Hiroshima and Nagasaki immediately raised questions regarding a future which could take two paths: a path to primeval devolution or a path to positivist evolution. John Hersey's widely read work *Hiroshima* portrays a world of humans forced to live by instinct; in other words, forced to devolve from human social organization to a Darwinian struggle for existence. Hersey describes the survivors being motivated by "an irresistible, atavistic urge to hide under leaves" (35). In Hersey's view, the aftermath of the explosion caused the humans involved to revert to a more animal-like existence. Describing one Japanese doctor after the explosion, Hersey writes: "Dr. Fujii hardly had time to think that he was dying before he realized that he was alive, squeezed tightly by two long timbers in a V across his chest, like a morsel suspended between two huge chopsticks" (11). Dr. Fujii had become prey, metaphorically a piece of food rather than a respected doctor. Post-blast Hiroshima was a world of survival, not of human logic. Because of the numerous casualties to be dealt with another doctor had to lose "all sense of profession" and become "an automaton, mechanically wiping, daubing, winding, wiping, daubing, winding" (26). Hersey's account of Hiroshima presents a view of a city quickly transformed into ruins and ruled by a basic struggle for existence.

While Hersey's account highlighted the devolution brought about instantaneously by the atomic bomb, the scientists' movement worked to alert the American public to the dual consequences brought about by the Manhattan Project. In *One World or None,* the various contributors portray a world where a utopia/dystopia opposition predominates. Harold C. Urey describes the outcome of nuclear war in the following manner: "not only may our own culture be destroyed by these weapons of mass destruction, but all civilizations as they exist in the world may be retarded and weakened for centuries to come" (58). Nuclear war threatened to plunge humans into a new dark age, yet the technology involved in such a war offered the promise of human society evolving to new heights. J. R. Oppenheimer, in his contribution to the volume, vowed that atomic power promised "rapid technological change" and "Promethean qualities of drama and of novelty" as well as "fantastic powers of destruction" (22). The agenda of the scientists' movement was to promise a utopia if nuclear power was internationally controlled, but a dystopia if individual nations retained control of its frightening power. In a work entitled *Must Destruction Be Our Destiny?* which shares this agenda, Harrison Brown fears a future of devolution: "we want to live, but we do not want to live in fear, nor do we want to regress to the status of primordial man" (16). Levenstein sees a bright future in which food, clothing, and shelter will be abundant due to atomic power and simultaneously a bleak future which is "haunted by the monster of its own creation" (8).[2]

Levenstein's monster represents a typical postwar way of conceptualizing the atomic bomb, as a primeval creature. In early reactions to its use,[3] references abound to the atomic bomb as a "Frankenstein monster." Laurence portrays the atomic bomb as a prehistoric creature. He posits human evolution as evident in the Manhattan Project: after the Trinity test Laurence describes the scientists in the following way—"Primitive man was metamorphosed into modern man—shaking hands, slapping his fellow on the back, all laughing like happy children" (12). Yet, witnessing the dropping of the atomic bomb over Nagasaki, Laurence saw the mushroom cloud as a prehistoric monster (238), and speculated that after a nuclear war, modern humans would devolve to an animal-like existence (174). Laurence's metaphorical capturing of the force of the atomic bomb as prehistoric creature reveals the evolution/devolution matrix within which atomic power was framed—a conceptualization that finds cinematic expression in *The Beast from 20,000 Fathoms.*

Eugene Lourie's *The Beast from 20,000 Fathoms* (1953) deals with an atomic-bomb test in the Arctic Circle that leads to the thawing of a prehistoric rhedosaurus, which makes its way by water to New York City, wreaking havoc as it goes, and finally doing so within the city itself. A physicist involved in the bomb test, Thomas Nesbitt, with the help of two paleontologists, Dr. Elson and his assistant, Leigh Hunter, along with the military, is able to stop the creature by shooting a radioactive isotope into a wound inflicted on the beast by a bazooka.

Beast immediately raises the question on many people's minds in the early fifties: will A-bomb tests bring about peace and progress or war and destruction? Discussing the test that reanimates the rhedosaurus, Nesbitt and his colleague Dr. Ritchie contemplate the implications of bomb testing. Nesbitt is cautious about speculating on the meaning of the tests because "mentally we [men] are still crawling." Ritchie responds that each test helps "write the first chapter of a new Genesis."[4] Nesbitt worries that bomb tests may be writing "the last chapter of the old one." Confirming Nesbitt's fear of nuclear apocalypse, when he and Ritchie examine the test site, the rhedosaurus emerges, kills Ritchie, and wounds Nesbitt. Nesbitt's account of his encounter with the prehistoric creature is at first labeled as illusion caused by war trauma by Dr. Ingersoll, a New York psychiatrist in charge of treating Nesbitt after the attack. Within the context of the film, far from being a psychological monster, the creature is real, an ancient force summoned by the A-bomb to remind humans of their precarious evolutionary existence. Conflation of a prehistoric dinosaur and the latest technology of the Atomic Age points to postwar concerns that nuclear technology may make humans like dinosaurs—a once dominant species now facing extinction.[5]

When the creature attacks New York, it wreaks havoc on the city much like an atomic bomb attack might. The creature clearly is being used metaphorically to embody 1950s America's worst nightmare/fantasy—the nuclear destruction of its largest city.[6] Describing the aftermath of Hiroshima, Harrison Brown notes that "one army officer remarked that the city seemed to have been ground into dust by the foot of giant" (4), and describes the demolished buildings there as looking as if "giants had shaken them vigorously, pulverizing their contents" (7). The rhedosaurus is just such a giant, one that can destroy New York skyscrapers. Further, when the creature attacks New York, it produces effects similar to those induced by an atomic-bomb attack. The creature drives people underground into shelters. It causes them to devolve, as panic makes them instinctually motivated. A crowd of panicked New Yorkers tramples a blind man. The creature's attack results in a state of emergency being declared in the city. The Civil Defense troops are called to help stop the panic—"Civil Defense" being a fifties byword for nuclear war with its widely publicized "duck-and-cover" advertisements. The attack by the creature is described in a newscast as the "worst disaster in New York's history." Whereas King Kong's attack on New York also represents a primitive past intruding on a modern city, King Kong is brought to New York because of capitalist greed; the rhedosaurus is accidentally brought there by a technology which no human fully understands or controls.[7] Further, the creature brings contamination with it in the form of a mysterious disease. A doctor treating ill patients says that the "monster is a giant germ-carrier." When soldiers shoot the creature with bazookas, the creature's blood infects them and causes them to collapse instantaneously. The creature's disease-ridden body metaphorically embodies radiation sickness, a disease invested with an almost supernatural quality in the minds of the postwar public.[8] The atomic bomb brings about devolution, as New York is thrown into chaos, and finds itself at the mercy of the prehistoric beast.

The solution to the beast's threat indicates the fine line between evolution and devolution that structures the film's representation of atomic power. While *Beast* undoubtedly questions the progress supposedly inherent in the bomb, portraying bomb tests as dangerous, as unleashing a primitive, uncontrollable force, the film also reaffirms the progress of the Atomic Age by making Nesbitt's expertise in the study of the radioactive isotope the factor that makes destruction of the beast possible. The circular logic of the film represents a paranoiac world view wherein problem and solution turn out to be one and the same.[9] However, the final image of the beast dying amidst the burning ruins of a Coney Island roller coaster troubles the progress implied in the ability of scientists and soldiers to destroy it because it references the burning ruins of Hiroshima. The beast becomes another victim of the Atomic Age. Disturbed in its frozen rest, it represents a primeval past of brutality, but ultimately a past which cannot match the brutality of a supposedly more evolved age.[10]

As *Beast* demonstrates, the ancient world and the modern world blur in postwar political theory. The brutality of the postwar age was frequently imagined as a devolution from an enlightened, evolved democratic form of government to a more bestial totalitarian political structure.

One way of maintaining an image of the United States as the most enlightened postwar nation was to project devolution onto the Soviet Union. The image of a backward, primitive Russia predominated postwar perceptions of the evolution/devolution matrix. As Ellen Schrecker argues, postwar spy hunts were predicated on the notion that only through stolen information could the Soviets compete in the nuclear arms race: "Otherwise, how was it possible for the Soviet Union, which was viewed as a backward, barbaric nation, to have built a bomb?" (32). In an essay entitled "How You Can Fight Communism," James F. O'Neil portrays the Soviets as people who use progress as a mask to hide their barbaric totalitarian impulses: "Next the salesmen and peddlers themselves must be skillfully disguised, deodorized, and glamorized. Hence Communists always appear before the public as 'progressives'" (qtd. in Schrecker 110).[11] For J. Edgar Hoover, communism was a disease that threatened to degenerate freedom, democracy, religion, and the American Dream. Exposure to it resulted in devolution. In Hoover's view, communism "reveals a condition akin to disease that spreads like an epidemic and like an epidemic a quarantine is necessary to keep it from infecting the Nation" (qtd. in Schrecker 119-20). This perception of communism as infectious spanned the political spectrum. In a 1952 campaign speech, Adlai Stevenson comments that communism was "a disease which may have killed more people in this world than cancer, tuberculosis, and heart disease combined" (qtd. in Sayre 201). For Raymond B. Allen, communists should not teach in universities because their totalitarian beliefs threaten the evolution of American democracy: "Communism would substitute a doctrine of fear, of little faith, and would submerge the human spirit to the vicious ends of a crass materialism" (7).

In a mid-1950s study which evaluated Americans' attitudes toward communism, Samuel Stouffer discerned a belief among the majority of the people surveyed that "*the less educated and working-class people were more likely to be communists than the better-educated and white-collar people*" (172). In addition to a belief in communists as ignorant, Stouffer related that 1950s Americans believed communists were morally corrupt, respondents labeling them "queer people" and "warped personalities" (175). In Harry Horner's sf film *Red Planet Mars* (1952), the Soviet Union is portrayed as a backward country. Scenes of Russian peasants living in one-room huts filled with straw serve to reinforce stereotypes of Russians as primitive and hence of communism as a political system lower on the social evolutionary scale than American democracy. Russian peasant equals Soviet citizen in the film's logic. A 1952

Life magazine article, "Iron Curtain Look Is Here!" satirizes backward Soviet fashion, subtitling the article "U.S. envoy's wife finds Moscow modes high priced, wide shouldered, not very handsome" (qtd. in Barson n.p.). On every level, Soviet life is portrayed as inferior to American life—from political systems, to shelter, to women's clothing.

Postwar discussions of communist totalitarianism as a degeneration of political evolution were inherited from nineteenth-century political theory. European imperialism portrayed totalitarian governments as evolutionarily lower and hence seeking enlightenment from democratic forms of government. Edward Said discusses European imperialism's perception of oriental despotism as "irrational, depraved (fallen), childlike, 'different,'" and therefore in need of parenting from European democracy (40). In the 1950s, the Eastern Other for the United States was the Soviet Union, the devolved, childlike primitive country that threatened democracy with depravity and degeneration.

Yet, the fear of totalitarianism debilitating democracy did not center exclusively on the Soviet Union. Fears of internal corrosion of the democratic ideal abound in postwar commentary. The secrecy of the Manhattan Project resulted in fear of the possible establishment of an internal police state, one that could summon civilians to work on an expensive and dangerous project kept secret from the American public. Thus, the fear of elitism and corruption at Los Alamos resulted in the portrayal of the scientists' lifestyles as depraved, a criticism typically leveled at Soviet and American communists. Eleanor Jette displayed anger at the public perception of life at Los Alamos as decadent. Commenting on an article written by Walter Winchell, Jette stated that "He depicted the Dorm parties as drunken orgies and hinted that the Atom Bomb was concocted by scientists lying on couches strewn with rose petals while they plied themselves with fermented grape juice" (122). The depiction of Los Alamos as a despotic, amoral Roman Empire of scientists was a common one. Laura Fermi, wife of physicist Enrico Fermi, commented on the lack of ethical consideration at Los Alamos: "They were so involved with their work and under such pressure of time that they gave little thought to what later became known as the 'social implications of the bomb'" (98). The Manhattan Project was popularly perceived as displaying the kind of amoral totalitarianism that was otherwise associated most frequently with the Soviet Union.

The fear of a postwar decadent society created by an internal authoritarian structure produced by secrecy surrounding the atomic bomb is a fear widely expressed in 1950s America. This theory maintains that looking outward for the degenerative force is futile because such a force is already debilitating the democratic structure from within, due to the prevalent atmosphere of fear and suspicion. In his veto of the Internal Security Act of 1950, Harry S. Truman wrote that postwar internal security is taking "a long step toward totalitarianism," the result of which is "to reduce the vigor and strength of our political life—an outcome that the Communists would happily welcome, but that free men should abhor . . ." (qtd. in Schrecker 195; ellipsis in original). Truman viewed McCarthyism as a force that was causing the American state to sink to the level of the Soviet Union. The president's view was shared by Lewis Mumford, who feared that the suspicion pervading American society would result in decadence: "We can posit the familiar forms of these regressive reactions: escape in fantasy would be one: purposeless sexual promiscuity would be another: narcotic indulgence would be a third" (*Sanity* 30). Mumford perceived postwar America as a world which had lost its sanity: "And the fatal symptoms of their [government's and military's] madness is this: they have been carrying through a series of acts which will lead eventually to the destruction of mankind" ("Gentlemen" 5). Mumford's view of a degenerated American state, devoid of reason and living for the moment, mirrors propagandist perceptions of the Soviet Union. In the 1950s, the fear of devolution into totalitarianism hinged on external and internal forces. For my purposes, I want to relate this fear to paranoiac fantasies of degeneration before moving into a discussion of *Them!*, a sf film which complexly captures American postwar fears of devolving from democratic heights to totalitarian depths.

One aspect of a paranoiac worldview is a perception that the universe is divided into forces of degeneration and forces of purification. In the post-Darwinian world, degeneration has often been aligned with devolution and purification with evolution. Schreber framed degeneration in a specifically evolutionary and sf context. Schreber's apocalyptic delusion relied on his perception that the degeneration of the modern world had resulted in God intervening in the form of rays. Schreber saw the Order of the World as an evolutionary one that selects out corrupt societies. In his view, the excessive nervousness of the world has attracted the rays of God, resulting in a purification of the over-excited world through its destruction. As the sole survivor of this holocaust, Schreber had to be the founder of a new race of humans. The world's excessive "voluptuousness," which Schreber gendered as feminine (as I discuss later) forced the Order of the World to destroy the earth and its inhabitants. Schreber believed that voluptuousness prevented evolution in both the individual and the species, and, further, could cause God to select out both individuals and entire countries (208).

This post-Darwinian paranoiac view of degeneration producing possible extinction of humans was reframed within the postwar era in a complicated way. The American 1950s, and especially sf films, accepted this logic, but posed the question: is the devolution being produced by outside forces (e.g., the Soviet Union) or is it being produced by internal forces (e.g., the social, psychological, political ramifications of the atomic bomb)? In a fictional rumination on postwar paranoia, *Diary of a Paranoiac,* Edwin Mumford created a narrator whose delusions of giant spiders and a giant rabbit are produced by a fear of moral and social devolution. The narrator's fear hinges on the perception that American society may be as degenerate as its evil Other: "We cannot throw ethics to the winds and then blame the Chinese and the Russians for doing the same thing. We cannot engage in sexual promiscuity and then blame our children for doing what we have taught them. It doesn't work. It doesn't convince anyone. Not even ourselves" (91).[12] Devolution, extinction, totalitarianism, giant insects—one sf film pulls together these paranoiac postwar fears.

Gordon Douglas' *Them!* (1954) chronicles giant ant mutations produced by the first atomic-bomb test, which takes place in New Mexico. After the ants kill an FBI agent on vacation in New Mexico, the local authorities (represented by Sgt. Ben Petersen) are aided in their investigation by the FBI (represented by Robert Graham) and two scientists (Dr. Harold Medford and his daughter, Dr. Patricia Medford). The scientists and the military successfully destroy the New Mexico ants' nest, but two newborn queens escape the nest and are tracked down in Los Angeles, where Petersen dies in the successful assault on the nest of the last remaining queen.

Them! imagines the potential eclipsing of the human species not by an archaic foe like *Beast,* but by a new species of ants, a harmless group of insects suddenly made powerful by radiation. To their horror, the humans find themselves lower on the food chain than insects. When the New Mexico ant nest is discovered, one ant found outside the nest holds a human ribcage in its mouth. The ribcage rolls onto a pile of human bones. Modern technology, which promised to make humans stronger by extending the life span—one supposed boon of the splitting of the atom that was lauded in postwar America was the ability to fight disease with radiation—has produced a genetic mutation that threatens to make another species the dominant one.[13] In Gramps' store, which has been destroyed by the ants, a news broadcast discusses the WHO (World Health Organization) eradicating human disease. The television's hopeful announcement about human biological evolution is made in the eerie, desolate atmosphere of the destroyed store. Elimination of disease makes little difference in a world where humans are prey to a non-human, but strong, intelligent, and well-organized species.[14]

Ants are particularly well suited to embody fears of the human race being evolutionarily eclipsed. The dedication, organization, and successful military tactics of an ant colony make human society look chaotic by comparison. In a short story entitled "The Empire of the Ants" (1905)—one of the unacknowledged sources for *Them!*—H. G. Wells imagines ant mutations in South America producing a race of deadly, intelligent, imperial ants, which leave human empires in ruins and which, according to Wells' narrator's prediction, will eventually conquer Europe: "I fix 1950 or '60 as the latest for the discovery of Europe" (16). The resilience of ants make them well adapted to an Atomic Age in which nuclear war is possible at any time. A 1945 *St. Louis Post-Dispatch* article on the atomic bomb warns that if atomic power is used for war and not for peace, "science has signed the mammalian world's death warrant and deeded an earth in ruins to the ants." In Kurt Vonnegut's *Cat's Cradle,* the only surviving life after the use of ice-nine is that of ants. Vonnegut describes the survival of the ants thus: "they would generate enough heat at the center [of the *ice-nine*] to kill half their number and produce one bead of dew. The dew was drinkable. The corpses were edible" (186). In the novel, the ants' ability to survive is the result of their cannibalism—in other words, it lies in their ability to adapt to social devolution.

While the ants in *Them!* represent biological evolution manufactured not by nature but by the atomic bomb, socially they embody devolution. The ant society, like the Soviet Union or like what many feared the postwar United States was increasingly becoming, is a totalitarian one. In a secret Washington meeting about the ants, they are described as "savage, ruthless, and courageous fighters." Dr. Harold Medford warns that the ants' dedication "makes man look feeble by comparison," and predicts human extinction within a year if the ants flourish. Further, in his presentation at the meeting, Medford emphasizes the use of slave labor among ant colonies. While the ants' totalitarianism may be aligned with the postwar view of degenerate Soviet despotism—Wells associates the ants with socialism/communism, commenting that the invading ants will "force themselves upon the attention of the European capitalist" (16)—the ants are produced within the United States, and point just as easily to American totalitarianism resulting from the atomic bomb. Eleanor Jette's description of the scientists' dedication to the bomb project points to this type of connection: "Los Alamos was like a giant anthill. The atom bomb was its queen and the Tech Area was her nest" (42). Dedication to the bomb project and to the secrecy surrounding the ensuing arms race threatened to make America a land of non-human worker ants, zombified much like the little girl found in the desert at the beginning of *Them!*[15]

The ants' totalitarianism is specifically *matriarchal,* and the issue of gender in the film is a central one, as critics have noted. Some critics have connected the ants' matriarchy to the film's commentary on the status of women in 1950s society; however, I want to relate the ants' matriarchal structure to a cultural gendering of progress and degeneration which the American 1950s inherited from Victorian social theory.[16] Sandra Siegel argues that Victorian studies of degeneration equate the non-European savage and the decadent European within a single category threatening masculine civilization and ushering in "the 'feminization' of civilization" (216). A degenerate society, therefore, is necessarily a feminine one. In Schreber's *Memoirs,* he, too, connects to the feminine the devolutionary elements in *fin-de-siècle* society that call forth apocalyptic destruction. In Schreber's delusion, degeneration throughout the universe, which results in God selecting-out corrupt planets, is predicated on sensual excess, which, in Schreber's view, is gendered feminine (72-73). When Schreber believed he was being transformed into a woman in order to propagate a new race, he feared his devolution into sensuality: when he was transforming, voices asked him: " 'Are you not ashamed in front of your wife,' or still more vulgarly: 'Fancy a person who was a *Senatspräsident* allowing himself to be f . . . .d?' " (148 ellipsis in original). As Schreber's delusion makes clear, a sf framework extends to the entire universe the gendering of evolved civilization as masculine and degenerate civilization as feminine.

Nineteenth-century and 1950s' sf typically adopt this gendering of civilization. In *The Time Machine* (1895) H. G. Wells imagines devolved human society as the Elois, a weak, feminized, androgynous race at the mercy of the savage Morlocks. In *The War of the Worlds* (1898), the Martians' soft, sexless bodies have a feminine weakness that breeds their totalitarianism and dependence upon technology.[17] In *A New Species,* Robin Roberts argues that the equation of degenerate civilization with the feminine is a central one in the history of sf. Examining sf dystopias, Roberts argues that "the writers of these dystopian worlds evoke Darwin to suggest the awful possibility of Woman (as separate species in this formulation) supplanting and then disposing of mankind. In this regard, science fiction differs from the mainstream in its depiction of Woman as devolution" (9). Roberts argues that throughout sf fiction and film "a female culture means cultural degeneration" (36). The use of a matriarchy, in my view, takes place in *Them!* for this reason: choosing an ant colony immediately equates totalitarianism with degenerate feminine culture and thus begs the question that an organization ruled by a queen is necessarily a devolved one. Rather than dealing with the local level of the status of women in 1950s society, I believe *Them!* is utilizing a post-

Darwinian gendering of civilization and degeneration in order to explore the implications of totalitarianism within American culture.

On one level, *Them!* argues that the very epitome of postwar masculine civilization and its achievements, the atomic bomb, carries with it the threat of feminine devolution. While the Manhattan Project may be read as representing the epitome of a Newtonian/Baconian control over nature—the scientist as god figure who can master the forces of nature—postwar fears centered on the chaotic results stemming from this scientific achievement.[18] Radiation contamination, internal and external totalitarianism, breakdown of gender roles, dehumanization—in the postwar imagination all these ills threatened to undermine masculine rational civilization with feminine irrationality. The ants are produced by "lingering radiation from the first atomic bomb." They represent the feminine, degenerative Other that lurks behind masculine civilization. When Patricia Medford, Ben Petersen, and Robert Graham descend into the New Mexico ant nest, they discover a primeval world held together by saliva. Yet this underground world has been produced by the "progress" of the atomic bomb, and, further, is potentially the world of a new dominant species set in place by the Atomic Age.

The fear of the primeval, feminine ants results in American society devolving into totalitarianism in order to battle a totalitarian threat. As in *Beast,* the creatures called forth by the atomic bomb result in an American police state. In *Them!* martial law is declared in Los Angeles, as the authorities seek out the ant nest. The gendering of the ants hence serves to evoke a sense of masculine civilization capitulating to feminine devolution as a result of the atomic bomb and its physical and psychological effects.

Ultimately, *Them!* presents the atomic bomb as producing not progress but internal degeneration. And, as in *Beast,* the removal of the threat posed by the ants represents only a tentative resolution of the problem. When Nesbitt kills the beast through use of the radioactive isotope, the unspoken question posed by the film is if one bomb test called forth this beast, what about the numerous other tests? In *Them!* this question is posed explicitly at the end of the film. Graham asks: "What about all the others?" Harold Medford replies, "When man entered the Atomic Age he opened a door into a new world—what he will eventually find in that new world, nobody can predict." Although Medford's comment invokes the evolution/devolution possibility put forth by the scientists' movement, the focus of the film is on the negative results of the bomb, on the manner in which rational masculine civilization is collapsing under the stresses of the Atomic Age and becoming prey for another species. Contemporary reviews of the film indicate that the fear of being evolutionarily eclipsed was an urgent one in 1950s American society.[19]

Whereas *Them!* and *Beast* examine devolution produced by the atomic bomb at the political and social levels, Jack Arnold's *The Incredible Shrinking Man* (1957) looks at atomic mutation at the level of the home. *Man* tells the story of Scott Carey, an advertising executive who, due to a combination of insecticide and radiation, begins shrinking. The shrinking process is temporarily arrested by doctors, but begins again, and Scott becomes so small that he must live in a dollhouse. After nearly being killed by his pet cat, Scott falls into the basement of his house where he lives in a matchbox and battles a spider for food. Scott eventually kills the spider, but continues to shrink, moving on to a microcosmic existence at the end of the film.

Arnold's film focuses on the stresses placed upon men in the Atomic Age. Radiation and insecticide cause Scott to devolve physically, eventually becoming smaller than an insect, but his anxieties about living up to the 1950s masculine ideal are present prior to his physical devolution. If the 1950s American man was to epitomize evolved human civilization to set a good example in Cold War society, Scott's character reveals the stresses involved in embodying masculine ideality. In Richard Matheson's novel, on which the film is based, Scott feels insecurity about his ability to be a breadwinner for his family. He has gone into business with his brother at his wife, Louise's, insistence that he earn more money. The film emphasizes his dependence upon his brother as well. In the opening scene of the film, as Scott and Louise relax on a boat, Louise reminds him that "your brother provided the boat." Scott's inability to be a good provider plagues him prior to the genetic mutation he undergoes.

Once Scott begins shrinking, his fears of not living up to the masculine ideal become magnified.[20] As he becomes smaller, his social and familial status devolves into that of a child. From the conventionally normal status of masculine head of the household, Scott descends to one in which he is dependent upon his wife for survival. As Matheson's novel highlights, Scott's loss of masculinity is not predicated only on his inability to provide economically—in fact, he does do this once he sells his story to the tabloids—but is based much more urgently upon Scott's inability to be a lover to his wife, Louise. In the novel, Scott attempts to make love to Louise, but receives only pity from her: "They were the sounds and touches of a woman who felt only loving pity for a poor creature who desired her" (32-33). Scott is horrified because Louise turns from wife to mother in their relationship. She replaces their double bed with twin beds, and Scott shouts at her: "I'm not a boy! You can't treat my body like a little boy's!" (81).

While the film is less explicit in its portrayal of Scott's loss of sexuality, it, too, focuses on Louise's transformation from wife to mother. At the opening of the film Scott and Louise are portrayed as having a sexual and affectionate marriage. When Scott initially begins shrinking, Louise begins mothering him, offering him ice cream and cake in order for him to gain weight. One evening, Scott mentions to Louise his desperate need for her, but she rejects him, going to bed with their pet cat, Butch, instead. Butch's name is a reminder of what Scott should be as ideal 1950s man, and his inability to be the butch man of the house is underscored as Butch the cat replaces him in Louise's bed—and in her affections. Butch's brutal attack on Scott while he is living in a dollhouse cogently illustrates his devolution from 1950s man to plaything for his pet.[21] Like the humans in *Beast* and *Them!* Scott finds himself descending the food chain.

As in *Them!,* losing masculinity in Arnold's film means being plunged into a matriarchy. In Matheson's novel, the spider Scott battles is a black widow. Scott comments, "Black widow. Men called it that because the female destroyed and ate the male, if she got the chance after the mating act" (16). However, the notion of matriarchy as devolved system that pervades *Them!* is complicated when it occurs in Matheson's novel. Scott wants to believe that the black widow acts purely by instinct, and hence is not a match for his human intelligence, because, although he has physically devolved, Scott is still mentally sharp; yet, he fears that the spider is not all instinct: "he wished he could really believe that the spider was not intelligent, but driven only by instinct" (20). As I discuss later, Matheson's novel and Arnold's film ultimately work to undermine rigid notions of evolution/devolution, rather than reinforcing them as the previous two films under discussion do.

Arnold's film works with the notion of Scott's fall into matriarchy by making the basement a feminine space. When Scott falls into the basement, he lands in Louise's sewing box. Her pins and thread become weapons and tools that allow him to survive. A piece of cake that Louise has left in the basement while altering a dress provides the only sustenance for both Scott and the spider. Scott describes the basement being "littered with the relics of a vanished race," referencing Western society's move from matriarchy to patriarchy. In his earlier life with Louise, Scott resents his dependence upon her, but his descent into the underground world of the spider is not the negative descent into the ants' nests in *Them!* because feminine objects help Scott. Unbeknownst to her, Louise does ultimately save Scott's life. Further, the spider is not demonized as a negative threat as the ants are in *Them!* Although Scott kills the spider, he does not hate it. His struggle for existence has made him see the kinship between himself and the black widow. He comments that he becomes ruled by reflex "as instinctive as the spider's."[22]

Although the film does not portray the matriarchal world of the basement as evil, Scott's reassertion of patriarchal dominance is a key aspect of the film. Scott's existence in the basement is portrayed as a caveman-like one. Scott wears a tunic that resembles popular representations of cavemen's clothing. The box of matches in which Scott finds shelter is the brand Firechief that references tribal organization and man's discovery of fire in prehistoric times. Scott's goal in the basement is to establish the rule of man. He says, "As man had dominated the world of the sun, so I would dominate my world." Scott's battle with the spider restores his masculinity: "I still had my weapons. With these little bits of metal, I was a man again." Ultimately, Arnold's film portrays devolution to caveman-like struggle as a positive experience that deepens Scott's awareness and restores his sense of manliness. It is the supposedly evolved world of 1950s America that causes Scott to degenerate physically and mentally. The stresses of the Atomic Age make him question his masculine role and also make him undergo genetic mutation. Plunged into a Darwinian struggle for existence, Scott comes to value his "man's brain" and intelligence.

Both the film and the novel portray Scott's physical devolution as resulting in mental evolution. Scott, the atomic man reduced to the size of an atom, gains a perspective of the universe he could not have gained as a 1950s middle-class businessman. He realizes that the evolution/devolution matrix within which the Western world has understood civilization and existence is limited. Thus, Scott believes when he continues to shrink he will become nonexistent, but discovers instead that he will become part of microcosmic worlds hitherto unanticipated. He leaves behind a classical scientific view of a closed universe hierarchically arranged and enters an open universe which is made up of worlds within worlds.[23] In the film, Scott says he "had presumed upon nature" by believing his existence would end when his recognizable human form disappeared. Importantly, movement into these microcosms is not conceived of as a downward movement. In the novel, Matheson describes Scott's reaction to his new existence in the following manner: "It frightened him at first. The idea of going on endlessly through one level of dimension after another was alien. Then he thought: If nature existed on endless levels, so also might intelligence" (188). *The Incredible Shrinking Man* hence breaks with post-Darwinian notions of evolution and devolution bequeathed by the Victorians to the twentieth century on social, biological, and cosmic levels.

While *The Beast from 20,000 Fathoms, Them!*, and *The Incredible Shrinking Man* all focus on the ills of the Atomic Age, highlighting a paranoiac world-view wherein the effects of the bomb create monstrous results, *Man* focuses on the philosophical gains of living in an age when the importance of the individual life has been diminished. While *Beast* and *Them!* hint at an America devolving due to internal insecurities and atomic fallout, *Man* finds an opportunity for philosophical growth in the postwar period. In the worlds of *Beast* and *Them!* devolution means losing humanity, being eclipsed by an old bestial threat or a new totalitarian mindless one. In *Man,* physical and social devolution provide an opportunity for mental evolution. The civilized man of the *Atomic Age* may find himself in a Darwinian struggle for existence, but in the process he may also develop important new insights about the universe.

Man ultimately suggests that only by being outside the dominant masculine role can Scott see the Atomic Age with any kind of balanced perspective. In the following chapter, I examine one of the most famous outsiders of 1950s B-films—the creature from the black lagoon. While Arnold's *Man* affirms the outsider's perspective as more insightful, his two creature films sexualize and romanticize the outsider as an alternative to the non-committal and anxiety-ridden men who hide behind the ideal image of the man of the Atomic Age.

6

THE BOMB AND SEXUALITY:
CREATURE FROM THE BLACK LAGOON
AND REVENGE OF THE CREATURE

One of the most puzzling and intriguing aspects of postwar perceptions of the Bomb lies in its sexualization. Popular music, fashion, fiction, and film all invested the Bomb with a glamorous and primal
sexuality. Sexual desire and desire for apocalypse become conflated in
perceptions of the Bomb and in nuclear war fantasies. In postwar Bomb
fantasies, as in paranoiac delusions, sexuality becomes a means of containing the fear of the limits of meaning. While most 1950s sf films
create paranoiac worlds curiously drained of sexuality, a characteristic
some critics see as symptomatic of sf in general,[1] two classic 1950s B-
films are saturated with sexuality and its connection to the atomic age—
Jack Arnold's films *Creature from the Black Lagoon* (1954) and *Revenge
of the Creature* (1955). These two films create complicated metaphorical
links between the Bomb, sexuality and gender, and paranoia.

Postwar culture immediately associated the power of the Atomic
Bomb with sexual power. French fashion designers used the occasion of
the Bikini bomb tests to coin a name for a daring new bathing suit. Rita
Hayworth's picture was stenciled onto the shell of one Bikini bomb.[2] A
1945 *Life* photo essay promoted an MGM starlet, Linda Christians, as
the "Anatomic Bomb." The uncanny lead-photo of Christians posed her
as a poolside corpse, suggesting a sexualization of death present in the
eroticization of the Bomb. Popular music of the postwar period also
sexualized nuclear apocalypse. In the song "Thirteen Women," by Bill
Haley and the Comets, nuclear war is something to be desired because,
the narrator of the song tells us, it results in a ratio of thirteen women to
one man. Other songs, such as "Atomic Bomb Baby" glorified nuclear
war as a sexual experience.[3] What these examples and others speak to is
a covert desire for nuclear war as a sexual experience, as a final climax.[4]
Barbara Freeman defines "nuclear desire" as a desire predicated on "a
monstrous engulfment of individual entities and identities," a process
she analogizes to erotic fulfillment (314). The erotic connotations given

to the Bomb in the postwar period suggest an association between death and sexuality writ large. What I want to suggest is that sexualization of the atomic bomb has worked on two levels in the postwar period: (1) it has bound the trauma of the unthinkable of nuclear war by placing it within the familiar framework of sexuality; (2) it has served as a process whereby individual sexual anxieties plaguing 1950s society could be reconstructed in a paranoiac structure and thus experienced as a collective crisis rather than as an individual failing. I want to articulate the Bomb and sexuality within the specific context of paranoia before looking at how Arnold's films explore these issues through sf metaphor.

Paranoia frequently has its origins in sexual problems. Freud's discussion of Schreber theorizes that paranoia is the result of repressed homosexual desire that re-emerges in hallucinatory form. Many theorists dispute the exclusive association of paranoia with homosexual desire, which Freud makes, and, rather, see paranoia as a disorder stemming from sexual and gender confusion.[6] Schreber's paranoiac delusions may be traced to various sexual anxieties such as his inability to father a living child, his guilt over masturbation, and his uncertainty about his capability to assume the proper masculine role in his society.[7] Case studies of paranoia do, however, reveal that sexual anxiety is a precondition for paranoia. Sandor Ferenczi's studies of paranoiac patients reveal a man who believed in delusions that his wife drained his energy vampirically due to her sexual lasciviousness (159). A woman Ferenczi discusses found in the newspapers accusations of her own moral weaknesses and her husband's infidelities (165).[8] Indeed, many paranoiac delusions begin with individual sexual suspicions and gradually evolve into complete paranoiac delusional systems.

I am interested in the way that postwar cultural paranoia used the sexualized bomb both as a means of averting individual sexual problems and as a means of binding mass trauma.[9] Russell Meares discusses paranoia as an anxiety-reducing process that gives shape to a "formless terror" (663). Sexualizing the Bomb gives the unnamable apocalyptic terror a familiar and attractive shape and also provides a means of foreclosing on issues of sexuality and gender plaguing 1950s America.

Creature from the Black Lagoon plays out this very tension as the gill-man embodies the formless terror of nuclear holocaust and the Bomb and serves as a fantasy man who can fill the void of what the film perceives as a failed masculinity in 1950s society. At first glance, the film seems to have no direct connections to the Atomic Age. With its remote setting in the Amazon, it appears to remove itself from a 1950s society saturated with nuclear technology and mythology. There are, however, covert references to atomic anxieties sprinkled throughout the film. In *Creature,* David Reed makes analogies between the study of Amazonian fossils and life and space research. David maintains that his research is important because it teaches humans the process of adaptation, one which humans need to know about in order to travel to other planets and adjust to new conditions. The unspoken fear that motivates David's emphasis on adaptation is that humans will be forced to adapt to another planet or to a radically changed earth when nuclear war takes place. The creature himself embodies just this fear. On one level, he may be read as a mutated human, a preview of postholocaust humanity. On another level, he stands as a metaphor for the Bomb itself.

William L Laurence struggled to create metaphors that could capture the power of the A-bomb. Laurence kept coming back to descriptions that invoke the monstrous and the primal. For example, he described the Nagasaki mushroom cloud as a primitive, savage totem pole (271). Thus, the primal, strong, instinctive creature may be associated with the primal force of the Bomb, a force that was sexualized, as the creature is, especially through Kay Lawrence's erotic fascination with him. Further, the scientists travel on the boat *Rita,* which references the Bikini test and the eroticization of the Bomb through Rita Hayworth's picture. Julie Adams, who plays the glamorous Kay, bears more than a passing resemblance to Rita Hayworth.

Additionally, the tension between the creature as scientific fact and as superstition plays out popular perceptions of the Bomb as a scientific creation possessing supernatural qualities. Laurence, for example, who understood the physics of the Bomb, still relied on metaphors of the supernatural to describe its power: "one somehow crossed the border between reality and non-reality and felt oneself in the presence of the supranatural" (224).[10] The creature is associated with the supernatural through the Amazonian legends Captain Lucas tells to the scientists. Most explicitly, however, the film links the creature with a vampire through his inability to tolerate light; his deadly grip, which most frequently strikes men's necks; his inability to be captured on film; the bat which appears in his underwater cave; his resurrections from the dead; and, most importantly, his ability to seduce human women. On this metaphorical level the creature, like many of the monsters and mutants that populate 1950s sf, gives form to the unspeakable terror of nuclear war, binding its traumatic affect through a paranoiac delusion.

On another level, however, the creature serves as an answer to the perceived failure of 1950s masculinity, a failure that has origins in the very stresses brought to bear on gender roles due to the A-bomb and its impact on American society. In a move which has all the markings of paranoiac logic, the creature stands for both the problem (the Bomb, nuclear war, the social implications of the Atomic Age) and the solution (a new man who can revitalize an anxiety-ridden age). The ills of 1950s masculinity and sexuality are addressed through the triangle that exists between Kay, David, and Mark Williams. The two men represent polar opposites in the repertoire of 1950s masculinity. David is the hesitant intellectual, and Mark is the aggressive man of action, yet both men fail to fulfill Kay's needs and fail in their dealings with the creature.

David is a new type of 1950s man, the man whose fear of commitment calls his masculinity into question. Early in the film, Carl Maia asks Kay and David, "Are you two married yet?" Kay emphasizes David's non-committal approach to their relationship, and David says he is waiting for Kay to get a raise so "she can afford me." David's unwillingness to commit to marriage makes him a highly suspect character in a 1950s film. In *Rational Fears,* Mark Jancovich discerns David's lack of commitment as crucial to the film, yet believes that the film does not condemn David's immaturity. Jancovich sees the creature embodying immaturity. I, however, see the creature as a different form of masculinity, one that the film ultimately sees as more mature. The creature is sure of his desires, can act instinctively, and shows the greatest sensitivity to Kay of any of the male characters. I don't see him as arrested at an infantile stage, as Jancovich does, but, rather as a man who is completely other from human men in the film. Barbara Ehrenreich notes that "the average age of marriage for men in the late fifties was twenty-three, and according to popular wisdom, if a man held out much longer, say even to twenty-seven, 'you had to wonder'" (14-15). Sexual and marriage handbooks published in the 1950s attest to this same suspicion surrounding men unwilling to marry. In a handbook entitled *Attaining Manhood: A Doctor Talks to Boys About Sex* (1952), George M. Corner associates unmarried men with homosexuality and with immaturity. This masculine "flight from commitment," as Ehrenreich labels it, has interconnections with sexuality and the Bomb.

The sexualization of the Bomb is complicated, because postwar American culture associates the A-bomb with both male and female sexuality. Edmund Wilson's journal for 1945 recounts that in a nightclub in Athens, an MC "jokingly" said to a female performer: "I wish you were the town of Hiroshima and I *la bomb atomique pour tomber dessus*" (qtd. in Boyer 246). Spencer Weart notes that postwar cartoons portrayed the Bomb typically as male (148). However, the "Anatomic Bomb," the routine stenciling of cheesecake photos onto bomb shells, and the female names given to bombs (such as Laden Maiden) also associated the primal sexual force of the Bomb with female sexuality. This is the association I believe *Creature* is making, one which complexly intertwines fear of the Bomb with masculine fear of female sexuality.

David's failure to commit himself to Kay is symptomatic of the larger failure of masculinity in the film. After exploring the river and bringing Kay back a plant he has gathered while unbeknownst to him being watched by the creature, David asks Kay if she wants to go below deck with him—a clear sexual invitation. Kay, instead, decides to swim, and in this scene her connection with the creature emerges as he swims beneath her and watches her, even hesitatingly attempting to touch her. Earlier in the film, our first glimpse of David is of him swimming underwater. At one point, David startles Kay as if he were the gill-man. David and the creature are doubled, yet the creature emerges as more sensitive to Kay's needs, and, ironically, as a better suitor for her.

Kay's uncertainty about David may be operating on several levels. First, sex and marriage manuals of the 1950s indicate that the most striking change in sexual behavior among postwar women was the high incidence of premarital intercourse between women and their fiancés. Ernest M. Burgess and Paul Wallin in *Engagement and Marriage* (1953) note that "the great majority of the women who had premarital relations had them only with the men they subsequently married" (330). Yet, as Burgess and Wallin note, premarital intercourse posed a dilemma for women because while there existed pressure to engage in it, female virginity before marriage still held great currency in the 1950s. Burgess and Wallin relate female uncertainty about sexuality with what most 1950s commentators see as the largest sexual problem of the time— female frigidity. They conclude that the 1950s woman "is conditioned to be sexually frigid" (696-97). Albert Ellis calls female frigidity *The American Sexual Tragedy* in his 1954 book. Ellis comments that women "become emotionally upset when they do and when they do not engage in some form of premarital sexual activity. They frequently turn out to be orgasmically frigid . . . on the whole, they seem to derive about one-tenth of the sexual satisfaction and fulfillment of which they are potentially capable when they and their mates are fully sexually released and mature" (72). Kay's qualms about her relationship with David, and about her sexuality, motivate her attraction to the creature. Thus, the creature may be read here as a fantasy object that potentially solves personal sexual problems: this is also frequently the function of paranoiac hallucinations.

While 1950s women were pressured by changes in sexual and gender roles, 1950s men were faced with open discussions of female sexual desire, which, I believe, contributed to the metaphorical association of the power of the A-bomb with the power of what was perceived as an explosive female sexuality. David's flight from commitment may be related to anxiety in the face of a redefined female sexuality. While many 1950s women may have been frigid, marriage and sexual manuals suggested that female pleasure was unequivocally as important as male pleasure. Corner advises boys that both male and female orgasm must be the results of intercourse (45). Joseph K. Folson in "Steps in Love and Courtship" (1955) tells his readers that "the human female, when not inhibited through cultural teachings, has on the whole as much sexual need as the male" (229). David Riesman in *The Lonely Crowd* (1950) sees this strong emphasis on female pleasure as one of the pressures changing masculinity in the postwar period. Riesman argues that the "other-directed" man of the postwar age places more emphasis on sexuality than his forefathers because he looks to sexuality as a defense against the dehumanizing elements in his world, yet sexuality provokes anxiety because of the radical changes in the status of women. Since his wife possesses full sexual knowledge and can now offer him all the pleasures the mistress or courtesan did in past ages, she can also "seriously challenge the quality of his sexual performance" (154). David's hesitancy about his relationship with Kay may relate to sexual intimidation in the face of an educated, beautiful, and sexual woman.

If David fails because he embodies the postwar lonely crowd, Mark, who is a physical man of action, also fails as a suitor to Kay. Although Mark ostensibly looks like the villain in the film—he is greedy, wants to kill the creature, has probably taken credit for Kay's research—he often displays more sensitivity to Kay than does David. When the scientists arrive at Maia's camp, David leaves Kay on the shore, and the creature almost captures her, but Mark remembers her, asking "Where's Kay?" while David has forgotten about her. Mark's obsessive need to kill the creature, a need David likens to that of "a big-game hunter," suggests that he understands the creature as a threat, as the suitor who, in Kay's fantasies at least, has replaced both him and David. Mark represents what Albert Ellis sees as a popular 1950s stereotype of masculinity drawn from the comics, "the strong-man, hard-as-nails, Steven Canyon type of hero" (205). David embodies more the "Dagwood Bumstead type" Ellis sees as the alternative masculine stereotype.[11] As Ellis argues, these stereotypes were being perpetuated by 1950s men who in fantasy and in reality attempted to conform to these roles. *Creature* tells us that both of these masculine paradigms fail, and, thus, Kay's desire must be directed toward the creature, who is both more primal and more sensitive than human men are.

Like many 1950s sf films, *Creature* frames the issue of atomic weapons within an evolutionary context.[12] The creature represents a possible course of human evolution, a gill-man who is aggressive only to enemies, who respects women, and who, because of his aquatic life, does not build nuclear weapons and threaten to destroy the planet. Simultaneously, the creature suggests a possible devolution of the mutated human after nuclear apocalypse. Kay's eroticization of the creature through wistful looks, desire for the creature to live, and feelings of awe that he so desires her makes the horror of nuclear destruction erotic, and displaces gender and sexual crises of the 1950s onto the fantasy figure of the creature.

Revenge of the Creature brings out more explicitly the metaphorical associations of the creature with the A-bomb, and explores Atomic Age crises in gender roles further. When the creature arrives in Florida from the Amazon in a comatose state, a radio announcer tells his listeners that the gill-man has created "the greatest scientific stir since the explosion of the atomic bomb." When the creature escapes from Ocean Harbor, the mass panic that ensues resembles 1950s projections of panic in the face of a nuclear attack. Yet the creature's power is less random and kinder than that of the Bomb. In the panic of the creature's escape, a young girl falls down and is trapped in a net. Her mother shelters her and the creature passes them by. The first object of attack for the creature after escaping the park is a car. Thus while the creature embodies the very epitome of postwar technology, he is also anti-technology. In both films, men fail in hand-to-hand combat with him, and only technology can harm him. While he provokes the terror of a bomb attack, he kills only those who threaten and harm him and hence possesses a morality that postwar people found frighteningly absent in the concept of nuclear war.

Lewis Mumford, for example, viewed postwar society as composed of a group of amoral madmen unaware of their mental illness ("Gentlemen" 5). The creature binds the terrible affect of atomic culture by forming the terror in the shape of a moral, sympathetic creature. In the film, the creature's destruction by Civil Defense troops further solidifies his metaphorical associations with the Bomb. Civil Defense films domesticated nuclear war by suggesting it was winnable and survivable, while simultaneously instilling extreme fear and hopelessness in those who participated in Civil Defense drills.[13] In *Revenge,* the Civil Defense troops ostensibly solve the threat of the creature, yet he returns in a sequel to the film. Tension between reassurance and threat in the figure of the creature is played out in both gill-man films.

Revenge works to make the creature more explicitly a metaphor for sexuality than he is in *Creature*. Helen's sexual attractiveness is made much more of in this film than is Kay's in the original. Helen is interviewed as she watches Joe Haynes attempt to revive the creature. The newscaster interviewing her comments on her beauty, and Joe flirts with her as she tries to describe her graduate study of ichthyology. Both Joe and Clete Ferguson immediately make passes at Helen. During her first meeting with Clete, he asks her out to dinner, and the creature watches her admiringly. The creature kills two of his rivals for Helen's affections, Joe, and Helen's dog, Chris, and attempts to kill Clete as well. Discussing her pet with Clete, Helen says that Chris is "my one true love and favorite boyfriend." After escaping from Ocean Harbor, the creature emerges from the water just as a policeman is breaking up a couple necking in a car. The creature pursues Helen to her motel room, and gazes on her in her underwear. The creature emerges underwater after Helen and Clete kiss while swimming. Their sexual attraction to each other summons the creature again at the After Hours Club, when they kiss on the deck outside the club. The creature's metaphorical embodiment of sexuality is clear in the film, but whose sexuality does he represent? Helen's? Clete's? The Atomic Age's?[14]

While commentators frequently discuss sexual repression as a feature of 1950s America, contemporary commentators feared sexual *dehumanization,* not repression—a dehumanization that was explicitly linked in many commentator's minds to the A-bomb. Lewis Mumford emphasizes the personal as an antidote to a dehumanized and dehumanizing society bent on nuclear destruction (*Sanity* 60-61). Riesman also sees the fear of the dehumanization of sexuality as a factor producing anxiety among the lonely crowd (154). For Riesman sexuality is a last resort, "a kind of defense against the threat of total apathy" (154), yet one which is becoming commodified and dehumanized in postwar society. Sexual and marriage manuals contributed to this changed perception of sexuality. For example, Folson explains sexual object-choice to his reader by using geometrical designs to stand in for men and women (215). The creature is overdetermined as a site of 1950s sexuality. On the one hand, he embodies sexuality made monstrous, made non-human due to the conformity of anxiety-ridden society facing the threat of nuclear war. On the other hand, he is the organic, personal answer to the dehumanization Mumford and others are looking for. He restores emotion, sensitivity, and sexuality to an apathetic age.

The creature thus serves as fantasy for both 1950s society and, most obviously, for Helen. Helen, like Kay, faces the problems of changing gender roles. She is confused because she, like many women in 1950s society, must choose between a career and marriage. Helen tells Clete that this choice "doesn't seem right," and many 1950s sociologists agreed with her. Ellis saw women's frigidity as related to both an impossible sexual code of behavior and the inability for women to be both wives and workers. Folson recommended "removing all restraints upon the employment of women" as a condition for greater marital sexual satisfaction between men and women (239). Yet Helen is also plagued by Clete's non-committal attitude toward her. Prior to the creature's kidnapping of her, Clete has imposed a three-month separation between them to consider their relationship. Like Kay, Helen is plagued by the masculine flight from commitment.

The creature is a fantasy for Helen. He is a man who knows he wants her and claims her for his mate. He is sensitive to her. He obeys her command of "stop." He risks his life to bring her to shore and guard her, insuring that she doesn't drown. As Kay and the creature are doubled through their love of the water and their outsider status, so are Helen and the creature doubled. Helen feels sympathy for the creature's loneliness, because it mirrors her own. Her most significant relationship is with her dog. She feels trapped in a choice between work and love, and thus sympathizes with the creature's manacled body in the aquarium. As the creature is an object on display at Ocean Harbor, so is Helen. Joe and Clete verbally spar in their battle for Helen, and Clete says he is not going to "let Mr. America [Joe] cut into my cake." The creature is an object of tourist consumption; Helen is an object of consumption for Clete. Helen and the creature, however, fight against the commodification of sexuality, which Riesman and others see as a defining feature of postwar American society.

As in the first film, the creature's status as possibly superior to humans is framed in an evolutionary context. At Ocean Harbor, Clete's studies of primate intelligence make him wonder "if there is any difference" between human and chimpanzee intelligence. Further, Flippy, "the 'educated' porpoise" that performs at Ocean Harbor, also breaks down boundaries between human and non-human intelligence. Watching Flippy perform, Helen comments that "If Flippy gets any smarter, he'll start talking." The creature most clearly calls into question the superiority of human intelligence. When Clete runs tests on the creature, he concludes that in every test the gill-man "just misses being human." And that is a central point of the film: by "missing" being human, the creature possesses a potential superiority to what many 1950s people saw as a destructive and apathetic human race.

Arnold's two gill-man films thoughtfully create sf metaphors that intertwine eroticism and the Bomb.[15] The non-realistic frameworks of the films allows complicated issues of the atomic age to be explored on the only level they can be examined—the metaphorical one. Nuclear war was in the 1950s and remains today the unthinkable, the unrepresentable The last two chapters of this work engage the issue of the unrepresentable through explorations of how sf elided the issue of nuclear war through representing it both as the mythological and as conventional warfare.

7

FROM TRAUMA TO PARANOIA:
NUCLEAR WEAPONS, SCIENCE FICTION, AND HISTORY

The Atomic Age immediately perceived itself as a new historical epoch. Laurence recounted that the creation of the atomic bomb "marks the first time in the history of man's struggle . . . that he is actually present at the birth of a new era on this planet" (164). The Manhattan Project scientists echo this self-conscious awareness of a new historical age beginning themselves. In an essay written for *One World or None*, J. R. Oppenheimer labels the release of atomic energy as "revolutionary" (22). Yet, at the same time that postwar thinkers appeared to be periodizing the bomb as something new, they simultaneously worked to take it and its implications out of historical time and place them in mythological and eschatological time. Laurence, completing the thought about "a new era," closed his sentence by adding that we have "full awareness of its [the bomb's] titanic potentialities for good or evil" (164). Similarly, in the same article in which Oppenheimer labeled atomic energy "revolutionary," he also described it as "promethean" (22).[1] The Bomb and its implications were historicized only to be ahistoricized as Greek mythology. This tension between the apparent novelty of nuclear weapons and their apparent connection to continuous, ahistorical forces is one present in postwar reactions to and representations of nuclear weapons. In this chapter, after a theoretical introduction, I explore the ahistoricizing of nuclear weapons in three sf films, *Earth Vs. The Flying Saucers, 20 Million Miles to Earth,* and *The Monolith Monsters.*

I begin by articulating a theory of history as the traumatic that must be narrativized in order to be expressed. Trauma is that which is painfully experienced but which cannot be adequately translated into language or even translated at all.[2] Laplanche and Pontalis define trauma as "an event in the subject's life defined by its intensity, by the subject's incapacity to respond adequately to it, and by the upheaval and long-lasting effects that it brings about in the psychical organization" (465). While trauma is experienced at the individual level of the subject, it may also be experienced at a cultural level. Cathy Caruth argues that trauma "does not simply serve as record of the past but precisely registers the force of an experience that is not yet fully owned" (151). The past lives on in unarticulated trauma, trauma experienced by subjects and by the culture as a group. The bomb and its implications were first experienced as trauma in the cities of Hiroshima and Nagasaki. The postwar world attempted to put into representations and narratives the unrepresentable horror and pain that was the reality of the atomic bombings in Japan. In addition to the naked human suffering experienced in those cities, the philosophical implications of the United States' use of nuclear weapons were manifold. Commenting on John Hersey's account of the survivors of Hiroshima, Georges Bataille pinpoints a central philosophical issue raised by Hiroshima: "the death of sixty thousand is charged with meaning, in that it depended on their fellow men to kill them or to let them die. The atom bomb draws its meaning from its human origin: it is the possibility that the *hands of man* deliberately hang suspended over the future" (226).[3] And it is precisely this trauma—we (Americans, humans) are responsible for weapons of mass destruction and hold the fate of the world in our hands—that causes postwar society to, so often, take nuclear weapons outside of history.

Thus trauma becomes translated into the universal, the mythological, or, more appropriately for the postwar world, it becomes translated into paranoia. The world of the paranoiac is a delusory one in which historical issues are played out as mythic battles between good and evil. H. W. Brands, for example, discusses the paranoiac's view of history as one in which the world is divided neatly into good and evil, resulting in the conclusion that "Humanity's problems aren't the consequence of some abiding deficiency in all of us. Problems are the work of bad people" (38). Schreber provides a case study in historical time translated into mythical time through psychic mechanisms.[4] Schreber, for example, placed the historical specificity of *fin-de-siècle* German nationalism outside of a specific cultural moment, stating, "the Germans were in modern times (possibly since the Reformation, perhaps since the migration of nations) *God's chosen people,* whose language God preferred to use" (50). Schreber lists some historical events that he has been told by divine communication were determined by God, including the severe winter of 1870-71 and the destruction of Phillip II's Spanish Armada (1588) (47). Further, Schreber's complex delusional system translates elements from his society into universal truths. Historically, specific phenomena like German nationalism, anti-Semitism, the Kulturkampf, and others became part of Schreber's paranoiac cosmology.[5] In this, as a psychic defense mechanism, paranoia takes the sting out of history by draining it of its human responsibility and placing it in eschatological/ mythological time and space.

Postwar America's cultural paranoia performed similar work. Richard Hofstadter outlines Cold War paranoia as a re-defining of the historical as the mythological. Hofstadter argues that in the climate of postwar paranoia, "History is a conspiracy, set in motion by demonic forces of almost transcendent power, and what is felt to be needed to defeat it is not the usual methods of political give-and-take, but an all-out crusade" (29). Thus communism stands not as an historically specific political system but as an embodiment of mythological evil—pagan and satanic.[6] The postwar Soviet Union becomes mythologically great and evil. I. F. Stone astutely commented during the 1950s that American liberals and conservatives alike painted communists as "some supernatural breed of men, led by diabolic masterminds in that distant Kremlin, engaged in a satanic conspiracy to take over the world and enslave all mankind" (69).[7] If the Cold War was a mythological battle against a pagan/satanic enemy, then we (the U.S.) as crusaders had been given the bomb by God. We were not responsible for its scientific creation and its implications. Harry S. Truman expressed this sentiment in his 1945 announcement after the destruction of Nagasaki: "We thank God it has come to us, instead of to our enemies; and we pray that He may guide us to use it in His ways and His purposes" (qtd. in Boyer 211). Thus the bomb has "come to us" and paranoia has bound the trauma of the weapon.

Another reason behind the mythologizing of nuclear technology in the postwar era was that ignorance about the new scientific discovery caused people to search for a frame of reference that could make sense of the unrepresentable content of nuclear physics. The science fiction genre worked in the postwar period to frame radical scientific change within the structure of myth. Robert Jay Lifton comments on the need for prior representational forms in order to make sense of nuclear bombs: "In creating, in recreating experience, we need some prior imagery in order to do that work, in order to carry through that process. And there was precious little prior imagery that could enable people to take in the Hiroshima experience, the event of a weapon apparently destroying an entire city" (qtd. in Caruth 135). Lacking frames of reference, postwar society turned to myth to articulate the meanings of nuclear bombs. Curiously, even a genre that theoretically attempts to imagine the future—science fiction—more often than not placed the bomb in a continuous universal process. Philip Wylie argues that postwar sf authors were irresponsible in creating "a new and sinister folklore" that obscured the scientific facts about the bomb in favor of mythology (235).[8]

Paranoia performs the same process of creating ahistorical meaning to fill in gaps in knowledge, especially scientific knowledge. The emergence of paranoia in nineteenth- and twentieth-century society has coincided with an extreme valorization of science. Thus non-scientists experience helplessness in the face of an encroaching science and attempt to compensate for that by creating elaborate delusional frameworks. Schreber, for example, continually argued that his delusory system was scientifically valid, even offering his body up for dissection after death as "proof" of the miraculous transformations he had undergone (251). For the non-scientific postwar person, mythologizing the bomb provided a means of understanding it; of paradoxically making it more frightening by associating it with ancient evil, but also less frightening as it emerged in a recognizable mythological form.[9]

In *War Stars: The Superweapon and the American Imagination*, H. Bruce Franklin argues that twentieth-century American science fiction created a mythology of nuclear weapons that was then adopted by American policymakers. He states, "For fifty years, from the first atomic explosion in Robert Cromies's 1895 novel *The Crack of Doom* until 1945, nuclear weapons existed nowhere but in science fiction, and in the imagination of those directly or indirectly influenced by this fiction, including scientists who converted these inventions from fantasy into facts of life" (131). In Franklin's view the American myth of "the ultimate peacemaking weapons" that would lead to world peace under American hegemony directly shaped the nuclear policies of the United States (153). Franklin's argument suggests that the atomic bomb was born out of science-fiction mythology. Thus the re-mythologizing of it after the reality of Hiroshima and Nagasaki was an easily achieved goal. Even those Americans who made nuclear weapons a reality could not separate these weapons from the sf myths that had influenced them. In *The Way to Ground Zero*, Martha A. Bartter argues that the public reaction to the bomb "reflected traditional millinnialism, with references to holocaust, Armageddon, and apocalypse—terms that sf long had used to imply that an atomic war would be the last one" (113). Whether directly or indirectly, American drew on sf-fashioned mythology to understand the nuclear threat.

Yet it was not ignorance alone that caused postwar America and postwar sf to turn to the mythological as a means to put the trauma of the nuclear into narrative, because those who did understand the science, like Oppenheimer, made similar moves. If the bomb is outside history, then belief in the positivist notion of history, so dear to sf and to postwar America, can continue.[10] As Georg Lukacs argues, nineteenth-century positivism worked to ahistoricize events while it simultaneously purported to offer a new theory of history. Lukacs argues that in positivism, "history is negated in a reactionary fashion and dissolved partly into an ahistorical system of sociological 'laws,' partly into a mystified philosophy of history, in essence just as ahistorical" (176).[11] How can a weapon that may destroy the earth be assimilated into a positivist notion of American history? Only by culturally removing it from a notion of historical progress can the nuclear be represented.

1950s sf films were one of the most accessible forms of the postwar mythologizing of nuclear war. The 1950s were the heyday for the B science-fiction film. In a 1956 review of *Earth Vs. The Flying Saucers*, *BoxOffice* magazine (a publication aimed at theater owners and managers) comments that the films "should encounter no difficulty in satisfying the patrons of most theaters and should prove potent in attracting many customers" ("Earth"). 1956—the release date for *Earth Vs. The Flying Saucers*—was the first "boom year" for sf film. That year saw twenty-five sf films released. Thirty-four sf films were released in 1957 (including *20 Million Miles to Earth* and *The Monolith Monsters*), and thirty-six in 1958 (B. Warren xv).

Fred F. Sears' *Earth Vs. The Flying Saucers* (1956) uses science fiction to displace nuclear technology onto an ancient alien race that threatens to take over the earth. The film opens by framing its topics as those that are part of a universal process. The narrator tells us that "since Biblical times" humans have speculated on visitors from another world. The opening of the film joins this universality with a paranoiac outlook as the prevalence of UFO sightings is shown throughout the world, culminating in a scene at the Hemispheric Defense Command Headquarters in Colorado Springs, which has issued the command that military forces are to fire at UFOs on sight. *Earth* encourages its audience to displace its trauma over nuclear weapons onto UFOs and, like a typical paranoiac delusion, uses technology to verify its system. Driving back to their work designing and launching exploratory spacecraft, newlyweds Russell and Carol Marvin encounter a UFO. Carol immediately affirms the reality of the sighting, but Russell is skeptical, causing Carol to reply, "of course it wasn't a saucer at all, I just shake like this all the time." When Russell hears the sound made by the saucer on a tape recorder into which he has been dictating notes during the sighting, the reality of the saucer is affirmed, as it soon will be to the entire world, which witnesses the invading flying saucers. Technology here verifies the reality of ancient prophecies and speculations about visitors from another world.

The aliens themselves are portrayed as an ancient force linked with mythological and apocalyptic traditions. They first appear to the earth in the form of St. Elmo's Fire, an electrical discharge named after St. Erasmus, patron saint of sailors. St. Elmo's Fire was already associated with the atomic bomb via Laurence's account of the bombing of Nagasaki. In an article published in the *New York Times* on September 9, 1945, Laurence relates that as the plane he was riding in was headed on its mission to Nagasaki, he noticed that the plane's propellers, windows, nose, and wings were illuminated by a strange blue light. He asked the captain what the phenomenon was. He replied, "It is a familiar phenomenon seen often on ships. I have seen it many times on bombing missions. It is known as St. Elmo's fire" ("Atomic" 217). At a barbecue, Russell, Carol and Carol's father, General Hanley, see the phenomenon, and Russell mentions that it was regarded as an omen in ancient times. Carol says that there have been so many around the project that those who work there have gotten used to them. Thus the aliens are taken out of time as they are perceived as the culmination of ancient prophecy. The film also links the phenomenon of St. Elmo's Fire with paranoia as the lights are eventually revealed to be paranoiac eyes spying on both Operation Skyhook and the new secret project developed to destroy the alien threat. A natural phenomenon, ancient mythology, and paranoia conjoin to make the aliens embody a threat that is clearly removed from history.

The film portrays the aliens as literally existing outside of time. When Russell, Carol, Major Huglin, and Sergeant Nash go aboard the alien spacecraft, the alien voice tells Russell to listen to his watch. He discovers that his watch and his pulse have both stopped. The aliens explain that their form of space travel happens between the beats of hearts and watches—that is, outside the boundaries of human time. The aliens' status as a mythological force not subject to historical time is further reinforced when they announce to the world that its inhabitants should look to the sun for a warning. They broadcast this message for twelve hours across the world. Prior to their invasion, an explosion takes place on the sun that creates floods and other extreme weather conditions, thus ruining communications and transportation. The aliens here clearly are being placed in eschatological time as they warn the world of an impending apocalypse, which they then attempt to effect.

The film also codes the aliens to embody the nuclear threat. Their ability to control the power of the sun is an attribute that links them with nuclear scientists. In an article in *One World or None,* Harlow Shapley traces the origins of nuclear technology to the examination of "the character of ancient sunlight" (8). The explosion of the first atomic bomb created an effect like a sunrise, inspiring Ferenc Morton Szaz's book title *The Day the Sun Rose Twice.* Laurence describes the explosion of the atomic bomb as possessing "the light of many suns in one" (10-11). Thus the people able to control the power of the sun in postwar America were really nuclear scientists. *Earth Vs. The Flying Saucers* associates the alien with the nuclear threat in other ways as well. The aliens are able to vaporize their victims. When they land at Project Skyhook, for example, they vaporize soldiers who have fired at their spaceship. John Hersey recounts a rumor that circulated around post-blast Hiroshima that a man and his cart close to the Museum of Science and Industry had been cast down in a shadow, the man frozen in the movement of raising his hand to whip his horse (73). Yet the aliens' vaporizing of their victims sanitizes nuclear weapons as the mangled, suffering, and dead bodies of Hiroshima and Nagasaki become (through interference) cleanly disappearing bodies. Further, the saucers resemble the mushroom clouds of hydrogen bomb tests, which frequently assumed a saucer-shaped form. When the aliens destroy Operation Skyhook, Carol and Russell are the only survivors left, a post-nuclear war Adam and Eve. Russell says into his tape recorder, "the air is becoming toxic."

The film not only translates trauma into paranoia by allegorizing the threat of the nuclear as one issued by ancient, mythological aliens, it also binds trauma further by rewriting the history of the Manhattan Project. After the destruction of Operation Skyhook, Russell works to find a way to defeat the aliens. He discovers that the aliens use sound as a weapon and decides he can create a weapon similar to the aliens' that can put their saucers off-course and cause them to crash. The government and military set up a "concealed laboratory" to which they ship supplies and send scientists. Therefore the secret laboratory at Los Alamos is rewritten as one that works to save the world from an alien threat, and one that bears no responsibility for its weapons research since it is merely mimicking its enemy. But instead of that enemy being a human one—build the bomb before the Germans do was the slogan of Los Alamos—it is an evil, mythological enemy, the kind of enemy that characterizes paranoia, one ancient and continuous, and in this case also one that clearly *does* possess the technological means to destroy the earth. In *Earth Vs. the Flying Saucers,* it is aliens who create burning ruins of destruction, not Americans.

Nathan Juran's *20 Million Miles to Earth* (1957) uses the mythological to displace the effect of nuclear weapons onto a prehistoric creature. The film immediately establishes a tension between timelessness and current technology, as an American spacecraft returning from Venus crashes into the sea near a Sicilian fishing village. The timeless quality of the fishermen is juxtaposed with the technologically advanced spaceship. Further, the film places responsibility at the level of the timeless. Pepe, a boy in the fishing village, releases the Venusian creature from its specimen capsule, thus causing the havoc that ensues. The innocent boy is responsible for the destruction the creature causes, not the responsible astronauts who brought the creature back, but would have never allowed such danger to run loose. The film works to allegorize the creation of nuclear weapons as the blameless release of an ancient force, a manner in which the creations of the atomic and hydrogen bombs were typically portrayed in postwar American society. Laurence, for example, analogizes the discovery of fission with an ancient, innocent discovery: "the discovery of fission may be compared to the discovery by ancient man of how to produce a spark" (38). America's discovery of nuclear weapons was, hence, blameless and part of an ancient, continuous process of discovery.

Additionally, *20 Million,* like *Earth,* displaces nuclear weapons onto an ancient, alien force. In several ways, the film associates the Venusian creature (known as "the Ymir" to the film's fans) with mythological time. Dr. Leonardo speculates that the creature is either a mutation or a throwback to a prehistoric species. It resembles a dinosaur, only it has a human torso. The creature and its threat are prehistoric, that is, outside of human history, and especially outside of positivist progress. The film also codes the creature as a mythological creature from the Greco-Roman system. Mythological sea creatures such as the Scylla and the sirens come to mind, especially with the Italian setting. When the creature wreaks havoc, even hiding in and emerging from the Tiber at one point, it appears to be a creature from ancient mythology reclaiming its old haunts. Similarly, the descriptions of nuclear explosions as prehistoric and mythical are a commonplace of postwar commentary. Again, Laurence provides the most vivid examples. For Laurence, the explosion of the atomic bomb is not only a Titan breaking loose, but is also "a monstrous prehistorical creature with a ruff around its neck" (238). By linking nuclear bombs with a prehistoric force, the film and the postwar world in general work to attribute safely the responsibility for and the effects of the nuclear to ancient forces beyond human control.

In several important ways *20 Million* codes the Venusian creature and its homeland as the nuclear threat. Thus when Col. Calder and his men crash into the sea, Dr. Sharman, the only survivor of the crash apart from Calder, is suffering from a disease that manifests its symptoms in skin that looks raw and burned. Calder tells Marisa that eight members of the crew have contracted and died from this disease. Sharman eventually dies from it as well. Radiation burns and sickness become naturalized as a disease that the astronauts have caught in the alien climate of Venus. The specifics of the creature also point to clear links between it and nuclear weapons. The creature displays a curious hotness. When it grabs at Marisa from inside its cage, she says that "its claw was so strangely hot." Hence it displays the heat of radioactivity, an idea further developed in its rapid growth rate. The creature grows incredibly quickly, and the scientific explanation the film offers for this is that the earth's atmosphere has upset its metabolic rate. A 1948 article entitled "A World Worth Waiting For" speculates that radioisotope experimentation will result in the ability to control growth in animals, plants, and eventually humans (34). Although the square-cube law has subsequently proven this notion incorrect, for the postwar world, radiation was often thought to presage out-of-control growth. Curiously, however, it is the earth's atmosphere that produces the growth in the creature, suggesting that fallout from atmospheric tests is so strong that it can cause an alien creature to grow to gigantic proportions. The creature feeds on sulfur to survive, hinting at an anthropomorphized bomb, a weapon that must feed off uranium in order to grow and become powerful. When the creature battles an elephant in the streets of Rome, a fallout-shelter sign remains visible in the frame as the two continue to fight.

Further, the film's Italian setting invokes Roman decadence, a conceptual category popular in postwar America, and one that sought to remove the social implications of nuclear weapons from historical time. The Venusian creature running amuck in the Coliseum and pursued by American soldiers sets up both an *opposition* between the American military and Roman decadence (here embodied by the creature) and as *association* between the American military and Roman decadence (since Americans have brought the creature to earth). On the one hand, in postwar America the Soviet Union was often metaphorically linked with the decadence and corruption that supposedly defined the Roman Empire. On the other hand, the Manhattan Project and the ensuing Cold-War structures of secrecy and McCarthyism were also metaphorically linked with Roman decadence. Eleanor Jette records that Walter Winchell portrayed Los Alamos as a placed filled with "drunken orgies" and corruption (122). Discussing the dominance of McCarthyism in the U.S. Senate in the 1950s, I. F. Stone notes that "one has to go back to Tacitus and the Roman Senate in its more degenerate days to match what happened here last Tuesday" (20). Psychoanalyst Franz Alexander warns in a 1957 article that the insecurity of American society may be a sign of decline, analogizing this decline to the fall of Rome (466). In a more recent commentary on the postwar world, Sanford Gifford argues that "the illusion of mutual nuclear deterrence" has made the world accept conventional wars as normal "like some of the nastier periods of the late Roman Empire" (25).

Whether the Roman Empire is invoked to describe the Soviet Union or to describe the United States—whether the creature in the Coliseum is them or us—the use of the Roman Empire as metaphor for Cold War policies again removes the issues of nuclear weapons and Cold War hostilities from historical time and places them in biblical, mythological time. The view of the Roman Empire as decadent is largely the creation of Christian commentators, who opposed the evil pagan world to the new, pure Christian world. Thus, accusing either Soviets or McCarthyists of Roman decadence removes postwar politics from history and creates a paranoiac opposition between good and evil. *20 Million's* creature, fatally wounded by Calder, then standing on top of the Coliseum, then tumbling to the ground, suggests that nuclear weapons and their ills can be defeated just as the ancient, decadent Roman world could be defeated by Christianity.[12]

Ironically, the epitaph of the film attempts to situate its story within historical time. Looking at the creature's body, Dr. Uhl asks, "Why is it always so costly for man to move from the present to the future?" While this statement may be read as evidence of the film's underlying anxiety related to the new weapons, the film has worked to remove the nuclear threat from both the present and the future by displacing the traumatic postwar present onto a prehistoric alien who is metaphorically linked with the Greco-Roman world. Thus the cost of moving to the future— the postnuclear world—has been so high that neither a present nor a future can be imagined.[13]

John Sherwood's *The Monolith Monsters* (1957) displaces the nuclear threat onto meteoric rocks that feed on human silicon, grow enormous, and wantonly destroy all people, buildings, and objects in their path. Like *Earth Vs. The Flying Saucers,* this film opens with a narration that firmly establishes the threat as an ancient, though continuous one. The narrator tells us that "from time immemorial, the earth has been bombarded by objects from outer space." Meteors are products of a force that can be traced back "from the beginning of time." "From infinity they come—meteors," the narrator reminds us. Yet in 1950s America, meteors did not possess the ahistorical meaning the narrator attributes to them. Eyewitness accounts from the Trinity Site recount that many of the civilians who witnessed the explosion there believed they had seen a meteor hit the earth (Laurence 195; Szaz 84). Hersey reports that when Father Kleinsorge, a Christian missionary, experienced the blast in Hiroshima, it "reminded him of something he had read as a boy about a large meteor colliding with the earth" (12).

Out of the dangerous radioactive desert, the monolith monsters emerge. The California desert setting of the film immediately calls to mind atmospheric testing. The bomb was first exploded in the New Mexico desert, and the deserts of the west and the southwest provided the most frequently used sites for the over two hundred atmospheric tests that took place in the United States between 1945 and 1963 ("Known

Nuclear"). When geologist Ben Gilbert brings a meteoric rock back to the lab for analysis, he puzzles over its composition, stating, "it just doesn't seem to belong." Local reporter Martin Cochran replies, "the desert's full of things that don't belong." Whereas the Trinity test and subsequent desert bomb tests resulted in unnatural radiation levels and contamination, *Monolith* works to naturalize the strangeness of the postwar desert by displacing bomb tests and fallout onto monsters ripped from the paranoiac imagination that has been "gathering the secrets of time and space for billions of years," as Professor Flanders puts it.

When Ginny Simpson takes one of the meteoric rocks back from the desert as a souvenir, the film invokes the popular souvenir from the Trinity Site—trinite. Martin expresses concern that tourists will pick up the meteoric rocks and spread the strange disease that has killed Ben Gilbert and has made Ginny seriously ill. Trinite is a greenish-gray glass that was created by the Trinity test when the atomic fireball made contact with the ground and fused the sand. For years after the explosion, tourists illegally gathered chunks of trinite to take home as souvenirs. In Socorro, New Mexico, a motel sold trinite to customers. A bank in Santa Fe made trinite a complimentary gift for new customers, and included the warning "do not hold near body more than 24 hours." Trinite necklaces were worn by women (Szaz 128). The potential health risk of contact with radioactive trinite is allegorized in the film through the mysterious illness that those who have contact with the rocks contract.

The Monolith Monsters deals with radiation sickness through its exploration of the strange symptoms the rocks produce. Contact with them results in the psychological reaction of zombification and a physiological reaction whereby the human body begins to turn to stone. Professor Flanders discovers that the rocks are parasitic. They absorb silicon from the human body, vampirizing it much like the effects of leukemia, a frequent result of exposure to radiation. Yet while the film raises the specter of disease contracted from radioactive materials, it defuses the psychic threat of this specter by associating the mysterious disease with the mythological. The rocks' ability to change flesh into stone recalls Medusa, Midas, and other Greco-Roman myths. Further, the film lessens the impact of exposure to radiation by suggesting that the mysterious disease can be completely and miraculously cured.

The film invokes the effects of atomic explosions in other ways as well. Rain becomes a threatening aspect of nature as water makes the rocks expand: they grow to alarmingly huge proportions during a rainstorm. As Hersey recounts, one of the postblast horrors of Hiroshima was the black rain that fell and caused eyewitnesses to exclaim, "The Americans are dropping gasoline. They're going to set fire to us!" (38).[14]

In the film abnormal black rain is refashioned as a natural rain that feeds a natural, ancient, and threatening force. The film emphasizes the rocks' destruction of livestock. Farmer Joe Higgins comes into San Angelo and reports that giant rocks have killed his livestock. His dog has been changed into granite. One of the most widely publicized of the phenomena surrounding the Trinity test was the cattle which had been exposed to the blast and came to be known as the "atomic calves." The cattle that had been grazing near the Trinity site appeared healthy, but a few weeks after the blast, they lost their hair. When their hair grew back, it grew back white. A New Mexico rancher also reported a black cat that had turned half-white after the explosion (Szaz 132). While the cattle remained healthy, their discoloration stuck in the postwar imagination as one of the eerie threats of fallout.

As in the previous two films discussed, in *The Monolith Monsters,* the Real of nuclear bombs is coded in the film, only to be denied by reframing the threat as an ancient, and here, natural threat. The meteors travel to earth, are aided by natural forces in their attempt to grow, parasitically drain the earth and humans of silica, and are eventually stopped by a combination of human agency and nature. After the rocks have been destroyed by the salt water released into the dry, desert lake, Dave Miller provides the epitaph for the film, "Martin, you always called that dry lake nature's worst mistake. It looks like now she knew what she was doing, huh?" The film reassures audiences that nuclear weapons are part of a natural, continuous process that has a reason behind it.

Moving from trauma to paranoia in postwar reactions to nuclear weapons means taking the unrepresentable horror of Hiroshima and Nagasaki—radiation contamination, and nuclear apocalypse—and translating this horror into the threatening, yet curiously comforting, black-and-white world of the paranoiac. History as the Real disturbs; history as myth allows society to perceive itself as part of a continuing and seamless process. While these sf films gauge the psychic impact of nuclear weapons, they ultimately work to make the nuclear threat mythological and even natural. Hence it becomes something outside of the bounds of human time and also outside of the scope of human responsibility. The final chapter explores how the postwar world further defused the threat of nuclear war by casting it as conventional warfare.

8

A BIGGER BOMB:
NUCLEAR WAR AS CONVENTIONAL WARFARE
IN *INVASION USA* AND *WAR OF THE WORLDS*

Along with the attempt to portray the atomic bomb as a radically new weapon was a perception of it as merely another conventional weapon that would be used in the next world war. While the radical nature of nuclear physics led some people to mythologize the bomb as supernatural, others attempted to tame the newness of the bomb by placing it firmly within the context of conventional World-War-II technology. Just as perceiving the bomb as a new supernatural force sought to remove human (and especially American) responsibility from the use of the atomic bombs on Japan, so contextualizing it as a conventional weapon worked to make Hiroshima and Nagasaki merely more powerful strikes in a world war and thus absolve the U.S. from responsibility for the new horror that the strikes on those cities represented. This chapter explores postwar society's framing of the atomic bomb as a conventional weapon by examining nonfictional accounts of the bomb and two 1950s sf films which perform similar work—*Invasion USA* and *The War of the Worlds*.

Official discussions of the atomic bomb analogized it with conventional bombs. The government- and military-sanctioned account of the Trinity Test was that the blast was the result of the explosion of "a remotely located ammunition magazine containing a considerable amount of high explosives and pyrotechnics" (Szaz 85-86). This explanation of the bomb's destructive capabilities persisted after Hiroshima and Nagasaki. The August 20, 1945, issue of *Time* compares the bomb to TNT: "The atomic bomb is more than 12,000 times as strong as the best improvement on TNT. One hundred and twenty-three planes, each bearing a single atomic bomb, would carry as much destructive power as all the bombs (2,453,595 tons) dropped by the Allies on Europe during the war" ("Politics" 29). The *Time* article wanted to emphasize the destructiveness of the bomb, yet used for its frame of reference conventional bomb materials. Truman's original announcement of the use of the atomic bomb on Hiroshima pushed the conventional weapon angle as well, making the A-bomb appear to be merely a bigger bomb. Lifton and Mitchell argue that this view of the A-bomb as merely a large conventional bomb prevailed because Truman and other official sources deliberately obscured the issue of radiation (6). Truman emphasized that Hiroshima was "a military base" and threatened further action: "bombs will have to be dropped on her [Japan's] war industries, and unfortunately, thousands of civilian lives will be lost" (*Public* 212). Truman's speech obscures the fact that this weapon is more destructive than just another bomb. The issue of radiation is completely ignored. Further, the bomb is made acceptable because it has been dropped on a military target, just like any conventional bomb during the war.

A further attempt to minimize the newness of the bomb came through analogies between the destruction of Hiroshima and Nagasaki and the fire-bombings of Tokyo. Karl T. Compton argued that the bombings of Tokyo were crueler than the bombings of Hiroshima and Nagasaki. In order to frame the bomb as merely a part of World-War-II technology, he asks, "*Was the use of the atomic bomb inhuman?* All war is inhuman" (54).[1] The official story of the bomb was that it was new, but only because it was more powerful, not because it brought new dimensions of human suffering via radiation contamination.

The military and the Project scientists were well aware that the atomic bomb was radically different from conventional bombs not only because of its destructive impact but because it introduced the new element of radiation. The declassified May 1945 minutes of the Los Alamos Target Committee reveal an awareness of the unique threats posed by the atomic bomb. The minutes show elaborate safety precautions prepared for the planes that would carry the bombs. Further, Oppenheimer presented information which recommended the safe distance that the planes needed to be from the mushroom clouds in order for the pilot and crew to avoid contamination. During the meeting, the committee discussed a plan for an incendiary raid which would follow the atomic bombing. The military favored the raid because "this [raid] has the great advantage that the enemies' fire fighting ability will probably be paralyzed by the gadget so that a very serious conflagration should be capable of being started." The committee rejected the proposal, however, because of the risk of radiation contamination for the soldiers executing this raid ("Minutes").

A declassified document detailing the radiation monitoring after the Trinity test also illustrates scientific awareness of the new, frightening dangers posed by the atomic bomb. Discussing Hot Canyon, which received high amounts of radiation dosage from the test, Col. Stafford L. Warren, Chief of the Medical Section of the Manhattan Project, comments that "Intensities in the deserted canyon were high enough to cause serious physiological effects." He notes that those who monitored the radiation took "considerable risks *knowingly*" and recommends that they not be exposed to radiation for a month (emphasis added). Thus the popular notion that the Project scientists were unaware of the medical risks of fallout is given lie to in documents such as this one. More disturbingly, Warren attaches a diagram that reveals a house containing a family with one child located .9 miles from Hot Canyon. The house received an unacceptable dose of radiation and Warren and his staff became concerned about the family's health. Warren compares the bomb's blast to "10,000 tons of TNT," yet he is well aware of the new danger ushered in by this big bomb. The American public's attention was focused on the conventional aspects of the bomb, not on the dangers of radiation.

A June 29, 1946, report compiled by the Manhattan Project concerning damage to Hiroshima and Nagasaki makes clear the fact that the concern over the two cities which resulted in government missions being sent there revolved around the novel aspects of the bomb. The two main purposes of the missions were: "1. To make certain that no unusual hazards were present in the bombed cities. 2. To secure all possible information concerning the effects of the bombs, both usual and unusual, and particularly with regard to radioactive effects, if any, on the targets or elsewhere" ("Atomic Bombings"). This same report highlights the Project's awareness of the differences between a conventional bomb and an atomic bomb. The report emphasizes the incredible heating involved in an atomic explosion, the duration of the pressure pulse that lasts a few milliseconds in a conventional bomb but lasts almost a second in an atomic bomb, and the amount of radiation emitted in an atomic explosion. The report details the gamma rays that release intense amounts of radiation and the ultra-violet rays that produce flash burns. The report denies, however, any long-term effects produced by the bomb, stating, "Medical findings show that no person was injured by radioactivity who was not exposed to the actual explosion of the bombs. No injuries resulted from persistent radioactivity of any sort" ("Atomic Bombings"). While the Project may have been unaware of the long-term effects of radiation, it was clearly aware that the atomic bomb was more than just a bigger conventional bomb.[2] The public, however, was carefully shielded from this knowledge.

Many of the major figures involved with the development and use of the atomic bomb expressed private and/or classified fears of radiation yet publicly obscured these fears in order to reassure the American public that the atomic bomb was just an immense conventional bomb. In a July 1945 memorandum written to the Secretary of War, General Groves relates his experience of the Trinity test. He expresses deep concern over the powerfulness of the bomb—"I no longer consider the Pentagon a safe shelter from such a bomb"—and over fallout. He comments, "Radioactive material in small quantities was located as much as 120 miles away. The measurements are being continued in order to have adequate data with which to protect the Government's interests in case of future claims. For a few hours I was none too comfortable with the situation." Groves was fully aware of the potential health risks posed by the bomb and of the government's culpability in such risks. Publicly, however, Groves sought to alleviate Americans' anxiety about the threat of radiation. For example, he remarked in 1946 that anyone exposed to radiation "simply took a vacation and in due time became all right again" (qtd. in Szaz 128).

Likewise, President Truman's reactions to the bomb display a split between personal fear and public propagandizing. In his memoirs, Truman discusses the bomb as "a military weapon" about which he "never had any doubt that it should be used" (419). Truman highlights his belief that the atomic bomb was to be used on military targets only, stating that "I told Stimson that the bomb should be dropped as nearly as possible upon a war production center of prime military importance" (420). When Truman learned of the dropping of the atomic bomb on Hiroshima he was aboard the *Augusta* having lunch at the mess hall. He got the crew's attention and "told them of the dropping of a powerful new bomb which used an explosive twenty thousand times as powerful as a ton of TNT" (421-22). To the crew of the *Augusta* and to the public reading his memoirs, Truman portrayed that atomic bomb as a powerful conventional bomb that had been used on a military target. In his August 6, 1945, statement, he fashioned the bomb as "a rain of ruin from the air" which would be immediately followed by a conventional invasion, ignoring the radioactivity which barred US troops from compounding the bomb's damage with such an invasion ("Statement"). In his diary, however, Truman expressed an awareness of the awful novelty of the bomb. In his July 25, 1945, entry he states, "We have discovered the most terrible bomb in the history of the world. It may be the fire destruction prophesied in the Euphrates Valley Era, after Noah and his fabulous Ark" (qtd. in Ferrell 55-56). Thus, privately, Truman was frightened of the new bomb and clearly viewed it not in conventional weapon terms but in apocalyptic terms.[3]

The accounts that probably influenced Americans' perceptions of the bomb more than official pronouncements were eyewitness ones. Hersey's *Hiroshima* brought radiation sickness to the public's attention, yet he described the bomb in conventional terms as well: "It had more than two thousand times the blast power of the British Grand Slam, which is the largest bomb ever yet used in the history of warfare" (49). Some contemporaries were critical of Hersey's minimization of the radical differences between the atomic bomb and previous bombings.[4] More insidiously, however, in a February 1946 *Reader's Digest* article,[5] Major Alexander P. de Seversky, a well-respected aircraft designer, aviator, and special consultant to the Secretary of War, used eyewitness knowledge of Hiroshima to propagandize the bomb as just another weapon. In his article, de Seversky told his readers that he expected to see new, horrific sights of war damage in Hiroshima, but "to my surprise, Hiroshima looked exactly like all the other burned-out cities in Japan" (122). He buoyed up the TNT comparison by stating that "the effects here were analogous to those produced by the blast of a distant TNT bomb" (123). Deaths by radiation sickness were vague rumors in Hiroshima. He related that all medical and emergency personnel he spoke to "denied personal knowledge of any lingering radioactivity" (124). Further, he blamed much of the structural damage caused by the bomb on "the incredible flimsiness of most Japanese structures" (123). He reassured his readers that nuclear attacks are survivable and that the conception of the bomb as a frightening new weapon was a "hysterically imaginative" rumor spread across the globe (121).

Further attempts to portray the atomic bomb as a conventional weapon were found in accounts that linked it to older technological advances in warfare. In a 1945 article, Arthur H. Compton makes an analogy between the creation of the A-bomb and the forging of steel: "To Daedalus, steel was much more than metal for fashioning swords. It was the means of making men grow to greatness. So likewise science" (53). Compton's point in the article is that atomic power will force humans to adopt a community-oriented rather than an individual-centered perspective on America, yet he minimizes the radical threat of the bomb by comparing it to the forging of steel. Hollywood sought deliberately to contextualize the bomb as merely another step in the history of warfare. John H. Lenihan examines several postwar conventional war films that linked the bomb to a history of weapons. In *Bride of Vengeance* (1948), Leonardo da Vinci's struggles with technology are voiced in the language of atomic scientists. In a 1952 memo to Darryl F. Zanuck, film producer

Leonard Goldstein argued that the first machine gun "is the secret weapon, terrifying and unbelievable—the atom bomb of a century ago" (qtd. in Lenihan 168). In order to minimize the horror of the bomb, it is compared to weapons that the world has subsequently integrated into its wars. But for the analogy between conventional weapon and atomic bomb to hold, the victims of the bomb had to be portrayed through familiar images of war survivors.

In 1952 *Life* published a series of pictures of the victims of Hiroshima and Nagasaki called "When Atom Bomb Struck—Uncensored." The photographs, taken by Japanese photographers and banned in the U.S. until 1952, focus on images of suffering that are indistinguishable from those of other war victims. The photographs show a bandaged child being pushed in a wheelchair and a baby with a bandaged leg. The radiation burns in both pictures are covered so as to be unrecognizably different from any type of injury requiring bandages. Images of rubble that dominated early postwar American representations of the two cities are prominent in the *Life* display. One dead body appears in the layout, but is obscured by the rubble of a trolley. The death could have been produced by a conventional bomb or by a natural disaster. The images are primarily of survivors. A woman breast-feeds a baby. Both are shown to be superficially hurt. One photograph, showing an apparently unharmed girl, is subtitled "Lucky girl." While the layout does counter the humanless images of atomic destruction prevalent in the postwar period, the uniqueness of radiation sickness is elided, thus making the destruction of the two cities tragic, but no more so than a city hit by conventional bombs.

One motivation behind postwar America's casting of the bomb as conventional weapon was to avoid the guilt associated with foisting a new horror on the world; another, however, was to argue that nuclear war is survivable. The bomb shelters and civil-defense drills of postwar America were predicated on conceptualizing the atomic bomb as one that could be survived. As Jay and Elizabeth Walker Mechling argue, popular magazines of the 1950s consistently referred to bomb shelters as "air raid shelters" (131). Shelters and civil-defense drills both used as their model images of the London Blitz. Articles in popular magazines of the late forties and early fifties bore such titles as "You Can Live Despite A-Bomb" and "How US Cities Can Prepare for Atomic War."[6] Civildefense manuals, such as Richard Gerstell's *How to Survive an Atomic Bomb,* focused on superficial ways of surviving, such as wearing a hat and long sleeves to protect one from the bomb's heat flash (qtd. in Boyer 310). The survivability of the bomb is as delusional a perception as the exaggerated fantasies of apocalypse that also pervaded postwar American discussions.

The minimizing of the power of the atomic bomb represents a means of control through cultural paranoia. Paranoia is an attempt to make meaning out of unarticulated trauma. One means of creating meaning in the context of the unthinkable of nuclear war was to understand the bomb culturally as something contiguous with World War II. Patrick O'Donnell argues that cultural paranoia "can be viewed as the binding force of the nation or community" (184). While paranoiac reactions to the bomb vary in postwar America, the belief in shelters and civil defense—the markers of the belief in nuclear war as survivable—was a shared cultural delusion which helped many Americans to gain psychic mastery over a powerful new force. The atomic bomb was different from other bombs because it brought with it the possibility of world destruction. If one atomic bomb could destroy an entire city, how many would it take to destroy the world? The ensuing arms race would answer that question. Thus, the fantasy of world destruction was made real with nuclear weapons. Howard Levine and Bennett Simon argue that in the nuclear age, "What were once fantasies of world destruction and mass annihilation relegated to the domain of wishes, dreams, and hallucination, have now become all too plausible" (1). Paranoia answers the threat of real world destruction with fantasies that keep that threat at bay. As part of the cultural work of binding the raw affect of the bomb, sf films participated in this project.

Alfred E. Green's *Invasion USA* (1952) is a red-scare film that uses an sf imagining of the future to portray atomic warfare. The film focuses on a group of Americans in a New York bar who voice anti-government and anti-military sentiments. A Mr. Ohmen hypnotizes them and shows them a future nuclear war in which the enemy has bombed and invaded the United States. Although the enemy uses A-bombs on the U.S., the film portrays their attack through the framework of a conventional invasion. After being hypnotized, the people in the bar turn to the TV screen and a newscaster tells them that enemy planes are moving across Alaska. The Americans are unable to see the markings on the planes and do not fire. The enemy parachutes from the planes to the ground. These scenes are interspersed with stock (presumably World War II) footage of bombs being loaded on planes. The first strike of the nuclear war in *Invasion USA* is a conventional one. The potential World War III presented here looks suspiciously like World War II.

This notion is reinforced as the film codes the never-named enemy invaders as being like Nazi, Soviet, and Japanese soldiers. The enemy leaders are dressed in SS-style uniforms as we see them working on their attack plans. When the enemy first uses an A-bomb on a U.S. site, the president announces on television that "Another day of infamy" has occurred, hence linking the attack with the assault on Pearl Harbor. Newscaster and protagonist Vince Potter describes an A-bomb attack on Washington as being "like a modern kamikaze attack." Talking to his love-interest, Carla Sanders, Vince says, "The last time I really liked a girl, they bombed Pearl Harbor," reinforcing the association of this attack with the conventional one in World War II. Although the enemy is clearly meant to be the Soviet Union, the association of the Soviets with the Nazis and the Japanese makes this fictional nuclear war a conceptually safe one. World War III will be like the previous war, only on our turf. The explicitly Soviet aspects of the enemy, apart from the accents and language, come in the guise of World War II stereotypes about Soviet soldiers. Two enemy soldiers take a captured Vince to Carla's apartment. One gets drunk and attempts to rape Carla. Vince dies trying to save her, and she plunges to her death rather than be raped by the solider. The stereotype of Russian soldiers as rapists is one derived from World War II.

Even when the war becomes explicitly a nuclear one in the film, it is a sanitized version of atomic warfare. Initially, the enemy strikes military installations only, thus framing atomic warfare as part of a conventional military strike, rather than as part of the concept of total warfare emerging from World War II. The enemy drops the first A-bomb on an airfield. Vince is relieved that there were "only three A-bomb drops" on the airfields that day. The choice of military sites for the attacks also reinforces the American propaganda that both Hiroshima and Nagasaki were military targets. In his influential article published in 1947 in *Harper's,* former secretary of war Henry L. Stimson assured the American public that Hiroshima and Nagasaki "were active working parts of the Japanese war effort. One was an army center; the other was naval and industrial" (105).[7] Propaganda such as this obscured the fact that the A-bomb attacks were civilian strikes. For example, The Hearst syndicate papers focused on a hydroelectric power station as the target of the Hiroshima attack when, in fact, this plant was not harmed by the bombing (Lifton and Mitchell 11). Hiroshima was a target of little military value, was not a major port, and was bombed in such a manner as to avoid destruction of industrial plants; the Nagasaki drop was targeted at workers' homes, not at industrial points (Alperovitz 527-34). Prior to the bombing, the Target Committee's discussion of Hiroshima as a possible site focused on it being "such a size that a large part of the city could be extensively damaged" ("Minutes"). In the postwar era it was routinely believed that the people of Hiroshima had been warned of the attack in advance. The National Atomic Museum in Albuquerque, New Mexico, still propagates this false story by displaying a leaflet that supposedly warned the Japanese people of the impending attack.[8] By having the enemy strike military targets first, *Invasion USA* repeats this propaganda. Of course the enemy will attack military installations first because that is what Americans did in World War II. In the film, the enemy is ultimately worse than the U.S. because the enemy provides no warning and does, ultimately, target civilian areas.

The impact of the bombs is further minimized by the fact that the enemy possesses A-bombs weaker than those belonging to the US. Vince says that the bombs are "nearly as strong as the American bomb dropped on Nagasaki." Further, the President reassures the public that the more powerful American bombs will be used against the enemy's home at a ratio of three to one. Then, to illustrate this point, the film uses stock footage of conventional bombs being dropped. Interestingly, while the film weakens the Soviet threat by suggesting that Soviet bombs are less powerful than American bombs, it also exaggerates Soviet capabilities to engage in full-scale war. According to *The Bulletin of the Atomic Scientists,* in 1952 the United States possessed 1,005 A-bombs and the Soviets possessed 50 ("Global" 67). As is typical in paranoiac scenarios, the power of the enemy was exaggerated both in fact and in film. Thus, in *Invasion USA,* the enemy appears to have an unlimited supply of nuclear weapons. Richard Hofstadter argues that in the cultural paranoia of the postwar period, the enemy is a projection of "both the ideal and the unacceptable aspects of the self" (32). Thus the enemy in the film plays out the American ideal of mass production of A-bombs—winning the arms race—and the unacceptable—the use of these bombs on civilian targets.

The film works to further diminish the impact of nuclear war by ignoring the issue of casualties. The atomic bomb attacks focus on familiar postwar images of destroyed structures. Human suffering due to the blast and radiation after-effects is ignored. In one of the film's fictional newscasts, American survivors of an A-bomb attack on Puget Sound take shelter from enemy paratroopers, apparently completely unharmed as conventional wartime stock footage stands in for atomic war aftermath.

The most obvious example of the eliding of post-blast suffering occurs in the film's portrayal of an A-bomb drop on New York. Vince and Carla leave the New York bar and as they stand outside, the air-raid sirens sound. The enemy begins dropping conventional bombs. Vince shelters Carla—inexplicably, they remain outside—and says that this situation is "like London in the Blitz." The enemy then drops an A-bomb on a building in the center of New York. The building begins crumbling a few feet away from Vince and Carla. Rubble falls on them. A rescue crew immediately appears and both Carla and Vince emerge unharmed from the attack. The A-bomb is just another bomb, one that causes structural damage, but which is survivable, even when one is outside and a few feet away from the blast. Radiation is completely absent from the film's portrayal of nuclear war.

The film also chronicles an absence of radiation in nuclear war in scenes which portray the enemy as directly parachuting into sites which have just been bombed. When the enemy drops an A-bomb on Puget Sound, a newscaster, from a live remote, points out the enemy troops parachuting into the aftermath. The belief in the ability of troops to enter areas that have been subjected to an atomic-bomb attack was not merely a fiction of propaganda films. The deliberate exposure of U.S. soldiers to radiation in order to test the survivability of nuclear war is now well documented. Between the years of 1950 and 1962, the Nevada Test Site was the center of these experiments. During the Desert Rock I Test, the AEC (Atomic Energy Commission) endorsed the Department of Defense's suggestion that troops be stationed four miles from ground zero, despite the fact that the AEC imposed a seven-mile limit on its own personnel (*Human* 298). The exposure of servicemen to unacceptable doses of radiation in these tests was predicated on a notion that nuclear war would be fought on the conventional battlefield as well, a notion that *Invasion USA* propagates.

Ultimately, the film cannot represent death by atomic bombing. In the midst of a nuclear war, the main characters all die in conventional ways. George Sylvester, a tractor manufacturer, is shot when the enemy takes over his plant and he tries to escape. Ed Malberry is killed in a flood produced by the bombing of Boulder Dam. The enemy shoots Vince, and Carla commits suicide rather than be raped by the enemy. The film displaces death by atomic bombing onto more familiar forms of death. Further, the characters appear to be much more concerned with the issue of invasion than with nuclear war. The scenes of devastation shown by the film are those that illustrate the scorched-earth policy Americans are adopting by burning railroads, food mills, steel plants, and other sites conducive to enemy take-over. A general in Washington asks, "Could the bombing of New York have been a diversion?" indicating that the A-bombing of the most-populated city in the U.S. plays second fiddle to a complete invasion of the country.

Invasion USA raises the specter of nuclear war only to tame it as merely another conventional war—World War II played out in the American Theater. This same binding of the trauma of the atomic bomb is visible in a big-budget, well-respected sf film from the following year— *The War of the Worlds*.

Byron Haskin's *The War of the Worlds* (1953) opens with a documentary-style voice-over that explicitly links the alien invasion with World War III. The narrator gives a brief history of the first two world wars and concludes that the "terrible weapons of superscience" will be part of the war of the worlds. The film invokes the nuclear threat from the opening, yet nuclear war is subsidiary to the conventional ground-war fought between Martians and humans.

The protagonist, Clayton Forrester, collapses conventional soldier and nuclear physicist into one character. Forrester, who conveniently has been surveying in the hills near the landing site of the Martian spacecraft, is a well-known nuclear physicist whose picture has appeared on the cover of *Time*. Yet once the hostility of the Martians becomes obvious, Forrester sends for the military to wage conventional war with the aliens. The army sets up a bunker to battle the Martians. When General Mann arrives, he says to Forrester, "I haven't seen you since Oak Ridge," suggesting a happy cooperation between atomic scientists and the military. Forrester is an effective coordinator for the conventional strikes against the Martians and thus the film portrays the atomic scientists as pro-military and pro-ground forces. Doubts about the need for a strong conventional army were expressed by many atomic scientists who believed they would be futile in the Atomic Age, and who often hoped that the invention of the atomic bomb would spell the end of all warfare. In *One World or None*, Irving Langmuir states that "We may some day come to regard the atomic bomb as the discovery that made it possible for mankind to bring an end to all war" (52). Forrester lays to rest fears that the nuclear physicist is anti-war. He easily seeks out and cooperates with the military and hence the film, like *Invasion USA*, emphasizes the need for a strong conventional military, even in the Atomic Age.

The U.S. battle against the Martians is staged like a conventional war. Preparing to attack the Martians in California, General Mann says, "they'll probably move around dawn," suggesting that the Martians are waging a tactical battle against the earth. After the army's unsuccessful assault, Forrester tells Mann that this type of conventional defense is useless, yet Mann reacts by sending in the air force to battle the Martians. As the Martians strike targets across the world, a montage shows refugees fleeing as in World War II. Images of cities in ruins recall the bombed-out cities of wartime newsreels.

Although this war of the worlds is played out primarily as a conventional one, the atomic bomb enters the film's framework in controlled ways. The Martians' weapon is a heat-ray that is able to vaporize humans and buildings. Forrester speculates that the Martians are able to "generate atomic force without heavy screening." The aliens are, then, waging atomic war against the earth, but it is a controlled one. They vaporize three local California men who approach their ship with white flags. General Mann says that "once they begin to move, no more news comes out of that area." In a strike near Bordeaux, "nothing remains" after the Martians leave. Their atomic power kills cleanly, destroying all traces of bodies and destruction, hence making the atomic bomb a clean and acceptable way to kill in a conventional war. As Los Angeles is being evacuated, one scientist says, "they'll stamp the city flat." In *Must Destruction Be Our Destiny?*, Harrison Brown cites an army officer who saw Hiroshima in the aftermath and said that the city "seemed to have been ground into dust by the foot of a giant" (4). The Martians threaten to make a Hiroshima out of major American cities, yet suffering bodies are wiped away with their heat rays, and the painful dimensions of atomic war are avoided.

Within the context of the conventional war waged against the Martians, the U.S. decides to use an atomic bomb to strike a Martian nest. The film does acknowledge radiation when it tells us that the government has delayed in using the A-bomb against the aliens because of "radiation danger," yet Forrester and his colleagues are to go in right after the explosion to study the effects. The atomic bomb used in the test is the most powerful one yet, but the Martians are unharmed by it. One observer says, "they haven't even been touched." The atomic strike is merely part of a conventional war as in *Invasion USA*, and is not a substitute for the use of ground troops. After the bomb fails, evacuation is the next plan.

Ultimately, however, *The War of the Worlds* relies on faith as the only means of dealing with and controlling nuclear war. If the military and even the A-bomb cannot win World War II for us, God will.[9] Sylvia's faith converts Forrester, showing the film's subordination of science to the spiritual. When Sylvia learns that the Martians can conquer the earth in six days, she states, "The same number of days it took to create it." It is this insight, rather than the use of the A-bomb that follows it, that shows the course to victory in World War III. Like *Invasion USA*, *The War of the Worlds* suggests that nuclear war is survivable, only here it is because God will intervene to save faithful Americans from total destruction. In the second church Forrester goes to in search of Sylvia, the pastor leads a prayer, "Grant us the miracle of thy divine intervention." The moment Forrester and Sylvia are reunited in the third church he visits, the Martians begin to die due to their lack of immunity to the earth's bacteria. Forrester's conversion to Sylvia's faith is more powerful than any weapon, even a nuclear one. Upon discovering that the Martians are dying, Forrester says, "We were all praying for a miracle." Church bells ring out and the narrator gives us the moral of the film: "After all that men could do" victory came through "the littlest things which God in his wisdom had put on this earth." The Martians die not from the random force of disease present in Wells' novel, but through God intervening in the form of disease.

Both films participate in a postwar controlling of nuclear war by casting it as conventional, winnable warfare. Paranoiac visions of invaders—the all-powerful enemy of *Invasion USA* and *War of the Worlds'* Martians with their probing eyes and invincible machines— serve to raise the specter of nuclear war, but ultimately tame it. This particular postwar escape from the unthinkable of nuclear war was to make it thinkable: World War III will be World War II fought on American soil, and, as in the previous war, American military strength and American faith will allow us to prevail. Only a culture's delusional belief that nuclear war is the same as conventional war could lead an observer of Test Able at Bikini in 1946 to say, "Is that all? I was just thinking that the next war's not going to be so bad after all" (qtd. in Lifton and Mitchell 84).

CONCLUSION

Sf films of the 1950s attempted to represent the nuclear threat by utilizing metaphors that helped American audiences to concretize and tame the unthinkable threat of nuclear war. In this sense, I believe these films performed important cultural work by trying to embody the repressed horror of the Atomic Age. Like the paranoiac delusions they so closely resemble, they express both the deepest fear (the nuclear is everywhere, inescapable) and reassuring comfort (the nuclear is a recognizable fear in the form of such things as giant insects, uncanny doubles, and aliens from outer space). Even if 1950s sf was binding the trauma of the bomb—and it clearly was—at least it was not avoiding it altogether. Mark R. Hillegas argues that "What is really important about science fiction is that in its various genres, it provides an extraordinarily flexible instrument for social criticism, that it is particularly able to deal with the problems of life in a new age of science and technology, and that, at the same time, it is able to reach . . . a much larger audience than does most mainstream literature" (280). Even if many 1950s sf films seem comic to us today, they register the immediacy of the nuclear threat for their original audiences. If we have more sophisticated special effects to embody our fears of nuclear war, we ultimately have no stronger or better metaphors for doing so than those employed by 1950s sf.

The extremely popular film *Independence Day* (1996) re-invokes fears of alien invasion, a 1950s disguise for fears of nuclear war. Watching *Independence Day* on July 3, 1996, at a Dallas cinema, I saw one viewer even take up the suggestion of the 1950s classic *The Thing (from Another World)* (1951) and open the exit door for a chance to "watch the skies" and alleviate the anxiety the film was producing in him. The recent remakes of 1950s classics such as *It Came from Outer Space, Invaders from Mars, Invasion of the Body Snatchers,* and others suggest that when we do imagine the nuclear threat, we still do so largely through the metaphors created by 1950s films.

The pervasiveness of the nuclear threat is what these films metaphorically represent. In the Atomic Age, there is no place to hide. Thus, the small town and the city, the home and the workplace, the body and the mind, are all potential sites for invasion by the physiological and psychological effects of the bomb. The very pervasiveness of the nuclear threat makes paranoia the ideal system for expressing fear of something that is everywhere. Paranoiacs perceive each detail of everyday life to be part of vast networks. How does one conceive of a weapon that possesses the potentiality for global obliteration except by seeing it everywhere? The monsters, mutants, and aliens that haunt these films give shape to the formless terror of nuclear war and radiation contamination. Szaz relates that following VJ day, a U.S. general on Tinian asked to see a model of the atomic bomb. A physicist showed him a mock-up of the bomb, and the general exclaimed, "Do you mean to tell me that what went in that place you're showing me there made all that explosion?" The physicist confirmed this. The general replied, "You may believe that, but I don't" (173-74). How can a weapon that was in the purview of science fiction before the war be understood at all except through metaphors? A fifty-foot woman, a prehistoric monster, a giant ant—these make visible the incredible threat of the nuclear.

Certainly the metaphors these films utilize to represent the bomb are limited and diminish the horror of nuclear war, yet nuclear war is itself definable by its unrepresentability. Leo Botstein argues that "Total death cannot truly even be imagined; no myth appeared necessary for Freud" (301). Myths of total death via nuclear war are necessary now, but no less difficult to create. Paranoiac structures are conducive to this imagining because the paranoiac has always been able to envision the end of the world, with himself as the sole survivor. In 1957 Ednita Bernbabeu recognized that "the autistic world-destruction fantasy of the schizophrenic has become the potentially immanent reality of the atomic age" (530-31). Yet nuclear war is different from a paranoiac psychically living through a perceived apocalypse. Nevertheless, the responses to the nuclear threat, whether in American politics or American film, have been paranoiac ones. Blema S. Steinberg argues that nuclear abolitionists, nuclear hawks, and those who support defenses and safeguards against nuclear war all share a perspective "infused with elements of denial, infantile grandiosity, omnipotent phantasies, and a narcissistic pursuit of perfection" (159).

I believe that we have yet to find a way of conceptualizing nuclear war that retains the idea of powerful and perhaps total destruction yet avoids mythologizing the threat. 1950s sf films chart our early attempts to make meaning out of the unthinkable, to construct metaphors for representing the unrepresentable.

NOTES

Introduction

1. I am following Richard Hoftstadter's distinction in postwar American culture between paranoia as a psychosis and paranoia as a cultural symptom. Diagnosing postwar culture as paranoiac, Hofstadter comments, "it is the use of paranoid modes of expression by more or less normal people that makes the phenomenon significant" (4).

2. J. Laplanche and J. B. Pontalis define paranoia as "chronic psychosis characterised by more or less systematised delusion, with a predominance of ideas of reference but with no weakening of the intellect, and generally speaking, no tendency towards deterioration" (296). Edward Jaye effectively argues that paranoia and fiction have many similarities and that the more popular the fiction the more paranoiac it is likely to be. I suggest that film, however, can capture the paranoiac vision even more strongly than fiction because it can represent hallucination as filmic (i.e., visual and auditory) reality. Christian Metz comments that the majority of hallucinations "by far are the visual and auditory hallucinations, those of the senses at a distance," as in the experience of film (183).

3. Don Siegel originally intended *Invasion of the Body Snatchers* to end with Miles hysterically trying to stop traffic on the highway. The frame of the film as it actually appears represents an imposition on the part of the studio; it is not an accurate reflection of Siegel's original plan. See Guy Braucort.

4. Paul Boyer, for example, discussing the postwar period argues that "science fiction is best understood as a commentary upon contemporary issues" (258). Rob Latham, discussing *Invaders from Mars,* comments that sf "taps into our collective dreams and nightmares, condensing complex historical development into memorable images and suggestive metaphors" (206). John Brosnan's influential study *Future Tense* also sees sf as being capable of indirectly representing the horror of nuclear war, as does Peter Biskind's *Seeing Is Believing.* Vivian Sobchack astutely argues that 1950s sf films are "about science as a social force, as an institutional aspect of contemporary civilization . . . they are extremely cognizant of science as an arm of institutional power" (*Screening* 50). This view of the social dimensions of science as an area with which sf concerns itself is one with which I strongly agree. There are those critics who see sf's representations of nuclear anxiety as a means of containing the real effect of nuclear war. The most often cited of these discussions is Susan Sontag's essay "The Imagination of Disaster." See also, Albert E. Stone's *Literary Aftershocks.* See also Chapters 7 and 8 of this book.

5. Films such as *White Heat* (1949), *Panic in the Streets* (1950), *They Won't Believe Me* (1947), and *Kiss Me, Deadly* (1955) very clearly deal with paranoiac worlds related to the bomb and McCarthyism. A commonplace of *noir* criticism is that these B-films indirectly addressed the issue of internal totalitarianism produced by McCarthyist America. See, for example, the collections *Shades of Noir*, ed. Joan Copjec and *Women in Film Noir*, ed. E. Ann Kaplan. See also Frank Krutnik, and Alain Silver and Elizabeth Ward.

6. I am using "affect" in its psychoanalytic sense here and throughout the book. Laplanche and Pontalis define affect as "any affective state, whether painful or pleasant, whether vague or well defined and whether it is manifested in the form of a massive discharge or in the form of a general mood" (13).

Chapter 1

1. Carl Freedman notes that Schreber "with his estranging, self-consistent, paranoid world-vision is himself very nearly an SF author" (20). Freedman, however, does not develop this point at much length.

2. In "Psychoanalytic Notes upon an Autobiographical Account of a Case of Paranoia (Dementia Paranoides)" (1911), Freud notes the similarities between his theory of libidinal cathexes and Schreber's theory of rays, concluding that "it remains for the future to decide whether there is more delusion in my theory than I should like to admit, or whether there is more truth in Schreber's delusion than other people are as yet prepared to believe" (154).

3. Robert Lindner is best known as the author of *Rebel without a Cause* (1944), a work in which he pathologizes the delinquent teenager.

4. Elizabeth Auchincloss and Robert W. Weiss argue that paranoia illustrates "how as individuals we hunger for knowledge, demand control, struggle with passions, and above all, insist on feeling connected with other members of the human mass" (27). Carl Freedman views the paranoiac as having "an abnormally high investment in the hermeneutic practice" (16). Patrick O'Donnell views paranoia as the knowledge produced by a nation or community that allows individuals to gain "visible identity as historically unified subjects" (184). Marvin Goldwert associates paranoia with a search for teleological meaning. Edward Jayne analyzes all successful fictional worlds as paranoiac worlds.

5. See Lacan's "On a Question Preliminary to any possible treatment of psychosis," and Joan Copjec's discussion of the Lacanian subject as the paranoiac subject.

6. Paul Emil Flechsig was a neurologist who treated Schreber at his nerve clinic first in 1884, when Schreber spent six months there and left apparently cured of hypochondria. After being named Senatspräsident in 1893 Schreber was readmitted to Flechsig's clinic for seven months, after which he was transferred to the Sonnestein Asylum, where he was under the care of Dr. G. Weber

for nine years. He completed the memoirs in 1901 and they were published in 1903. He drafted an appeal, which led to his release from Sonnestein in 1903. He lived in retirement until 1907, when he suffered another breakdown and was sent to the mental hospital at Leipzig-Dosen. He died there in 1911, physically weak and mad.

7. Schreber divides God into anterior and posterior realms. He uses Ormuzd and Ariman, Persian deities, to represent these realms. Schreber's other view of the goal of the conspiracy is that it denies the Schreber race offspring. Schreber and his wife had unsuccessfully attempted to have children prior to his breakdown. For commentaries concerning the significance of Schreber's childlessness to his illness, see Freud, Robert White, M. Katan, and Niederland.

8. This use of "scientism" is derived from David Knight. The term points to culture's tendency to extend scientific terms and ideas to various areas of life due to the prestige and glamour afforded scientific discourse in the nineteenth and twentieth centuries. I am indebted to Bruce Clarke for drawing my attention to this term.

9. Some commentators point out the truth value in paranoiac discourse despite its delusional character. Enriquez notes that "paranoiac discourse, and this is not its least fascinating aspect, very often presents this double aspect of being at once a mad delusional discourse outside reason, and at the same time, a passionate and often pertinent denunciation of disorders and evils 'glaring within reality'" (119). Harold P. Blum comes to a similar conclusion about paranoia's ability to reveal social injustices (98). David Porush argues that paranoia is a symptom related "to the fear of technology" (106). While I agree that fear of technology and scientific discourse may be a factor in paranoia, it seems to me that paranoia is more characterized by a desire to participate in technological and scientific discourse rather than by a rejection of this discourse.

10. Victor Tausk was a psychoanalyst and a contemporary of Freud. Tausk's essay was read before the Vienna Psychoanalytic Society in 1918 and published in German in 1919. An English translation of it was published in 1933 in the *Psychoanalytic Quarterly.*

11. For example, the following science-fiction works are ones that deal with parallel worlds: Larry Niven's *All The Myriad Ways* (1971), Poul Anderson's *The High Crusade* (1960), *Star Trek* episode "Mirror, Mirror" (1967), and *Star Trek: Deep Space Nine* episodes "Crossover" (1994) and "Through the Looking Glass" (1995).

12. The name Schreber cites is Count Czartorisky, a man who, as he has been told by the voices, is one of the Eternal Jews. One vital recent area of criticism of the Schreber case has focused on questions of Jewish identity that haunt Schreber's *Memoirs* and Freud's commentary on them. See, for example, Daniel Boyarin, Jay Geller, and Harrison L. Gruman.

13. See Chapter 3 for a more detailed discussion of this issue.

14. Paul Boyer cites "mass sterility" as a central concern of post-atomic-war scenarios (69). As Jack G. Shaneen and Richard Taylor relate, Hollywood's first representation of the atomic bomb project, *The Beginning or the End,* contains a scene cut from the final version in which a crew member asks "is it true that if you fool around with this stuff (atomic equipment) long enough you don't like girls anymore?" (7-8). David Bradley, in his account of his role as "Geiger man" at the 1946 Bikini Atoll tests, relates that the primary fear concerning radiation of the navy crewmen at the test centered around sexual potency and reproductive capability after exposure (111, 152).

15. Szaz mythologizes the project as well, portraying the use of the atomic bombs on Japan as occurring because "the furies of history, wrapped in the garb of the Manhattan Project, had assumed a momentum of their own" (156).

16. In *The World Set Free,* Wells predicts the development of the atomic bomb and its use in the next world war. In Wells's scenario, the horror of the weapon leads to peace and world government. The novel was widely read by members of the project. At the Chicago laboratory, someone placed a copy of it in the laboratory's library (Weart 97).

17. Oppenheimer's wife also knew of the work being done and possibly informed McMillan. As Rachel L. Holloway argues, the fact that Oppenheimer had informed his wife and other family members about his work on the project loomed large in the 1953 hearing that resulted in Oppenheimer losing his security clearance.

18. See Cathy Caruth's *Trauma: Explorations in Memory* (1994), with special reference to Georges Bataille's "Concerning the Accounts Given by the Residents of Hiroshima." See Chapter 7 for a more detailed discussion of trauma and the bomb

Chapter 2

1. In Freud's view, the self-aggrandizement of the paranoiac stems from the libido withdrawing from the world, then becoming "fixed on to the ego" in order to further "the aggrandizement of the ego" (148-49). In Freud's view, the creation of the paranoiac universe represents an attempt to re-establish contact with the outside world. For further discussion of self-aggrandizement as part of the psychoanalytic view of paranoia, see Allen S. Weiss and Joan Copjec. For a recent discussion of the messianic aspect of paranoiac delusions, see Marvin Goldwert.

2. Other suggestions made by scientists include inviting a Japanese representative to the Trinity Test, bombing a military target with the minimum of civilian deaths, publishing the results of the Trinity Test, and keeping the bomb test secret so as to refrain from using the A-bomb in World War II (Alperovitz 189). In his eyewitness account of the Trinity Test, Maurice M. Shapiro covertly references the scientists' desires by commenting in a memo to Captain T. O.

Jones, "My impression at the time was that an enemy observer stationed about 20 miles from the scene of delivery would be deeply impressed, to say the least" ("Observations").

3. As Alperovitz remarks, most reputable historians, including J. Samuel Walker, chief historian of the U.S. Nuclear Regulatory Commission, now believe that the use of the bombs on Hiroshima and Nagasaki did not prevent one-half million combat deaths (7). Alperovitz's purpose in his study is to examine the disjunction between scholarly and military perceptions of the use of the bombs and the popular myth that the majority of the American public holds.

4. For discussions of the either/or fallacy as characteristic of paranoia, see Prado de Oliveira, and Norman Cameron. Cameron describes an either/or dichotomy of "pseudo-communities" of enemies and friends which is relevant for sf and for postwar America and their particular manifestations of paranoia.

5. H. G. Wells' *The World Set Free* predicts an atomic bomb used in a world war. The scientists' movement's belief that fear of atomic bombs would lead to world government is expressed in Wells' novel, and this novel was a strong influence on the movement. The novel was widely read by members of the Project. At the Chicago Laboratory, someone placed a copy in the library (Weart 97). As John Brosnan notes, in 1944 John W. Campbell, Jr., was questioned by the FBI after publishing a story called "Deadline" by Cleve Cartmill. The story dealt with the development of an atomic bomb and came too close to reality for the FBI to be comfortable (72).

6. See Edward Jaye for a discussion of the black-and-white morality of paranoia and the connections between this outlook and the heroes and villains of popular fiction.

7. In "Farewell to the Master," Harry Bates' 1940 story on which the film is based, Klaatu is shot by a "mentally unbalanced" man who cries that "the devil had come to kill everyone on earth" (151). The fact that Wise's film makes the shooting of Klaatu seem predictable, rather than the work of a madman, indicates the intensification in public paranoia from 1940 to 1951.

8. Krin Gabbard makes a convincing argument for the parallels between Klaatu and Christ brought out in Wise's film.

9. Albert I. Berger notes that sf heroes frequently "solved political crises with the traditional elements of charismatic leadership and violence far closer to the totalitarian ideal than to the democratic" (146). I think this generalization can be extended to Klaatu, who must use the threat of Gort to influence American political policy. Robert Torry provides an interesting analysis of Klaatu's use of force, arguing that there are analogies between Klaatu's threat to the American people and the leaflets dropped over the bombed cities of Hiroshima and Nagasaki (13). In Torry's reading, Klaatu embodies the threat of nuclear destruction that lay behind Truman's containment policy regarding the Soviet Union.

10. For example, see Prigogine and Stengers, and Luce Irigaray for sophisticated theoretical discussions of the ethics of science.

11. Raymond Durgnat suggests that the Metalunans may be read allegorically not only as the Soviet Union but also as "England and our other pretty-soft-on-communism allies" (261).

12. In a recent interview, Edward Teller, the "father of the H-bomb," uses the term "progress" to dismiss those who oppose nuclear power and question technology ("Interview" 3). He argues that knowledge of the hard sciences will necessarily result in support for nuclear power and technology, thus labeling opposition to weapons technology as ignorance ("Interview" 6).

Chapter 3

1. Susan Sontag's essay "The Imagination of Disaster" is usually invoked as the first work to connect 1950s sf films with nuclear bombs. While Sontag poignantly argues for this connection—"radiation casualties—ultimately, the conception of the whole world as a casualty of nuclear testing and nuclear warfare—is the most ominous of all the notions with which science fiction films deal" (219), she does not develop this point at any length.

2. See A. Constandina Titus' "Back to Ground Zero" for a discussion of government propaganda films about the atomic and hydrogen bombs. Titus details that even as late as 1961 an Air Force film "Flight" shows a pilot flying through a mushroom cloud and emerging unharmed. Joyce Nelson relates that ironically television was used to reassure the public about radiation while simultaneously dosing viewers with "certain bomb-like radiating features" (37). While officially, the public was being reassured about the dangers of radiation, privately, children growing up during the postwar period were terrified by the mysterious force of radiation. "Edith," a woman born in 1955 and studied by psychoanalyst Martin Wangh, relates that in childhood she "conceptualized radiation as a mysterious substance which could travel through the air, was fatal and could poison the food and water supply" (313).

3. Hersey recounts the difficulties in finding marriage partners on the part of the Hiroshima survivors. One woman, Koko, finds that her fiancé's father forbids the marriage to his son because she has been exposed to the atomic bomb (150).

4. One issue behind Schreber's paranoia was his inability to reproduce. His wife suffered several miscarriages, and syphilis was suspected. Schreber speculated that the anterior realms of God were conspiring against him to prevent the continuation of the Schreber race. Freud discusses Schreber's fantasy of being transformed into a woman as related to his desire to successfully procreate: "Dr. Schreber may have formed a phantasy that if he had been a woman he would have managed the business of having children more successfully" (133). See also Janine Chasseguet-Smirgel and Robert B. White.

5. This collection consists of essays published between 1947 and 1954.

6. For a discussion of suburbia in both Menzies' and Tobe Hooper's versions of *Invaders from Mars,* see Rob Latham, who focuses on suburbia as a place of conformity.

7. Finney's Collier's serial *The Body Snatchers* was published in paperback in 1955. Siegel's film has been remade twice, once in 1978 by Philip Kaufman, and once in 1993 by Abel Ferrara.

8. Wells expresses similar anxieties in *The Time Machine* (1895) with the polarization of the Eloi and Morlocks, to which *Invaders* is clearly alluding. For a discussion of the fear of social entropy as the result of collapsing gender distinctions as projected in Wells' work, see Kathyrn Hume. For a discussion of the trope of the one-sex body in late nineteenth-century Britain and postwar America, see Hendershot.

9. For a good discussion of postwar gender crisis as the result of war trauma, see Silverman.

10. Barry K. Grant comments also on the lack of closure in *Invaders,* stating that "the narrative resists closure, unlike the conventional science fiction climax wherein science is redeemed" (81).

11. Hoberman cites these titles as indications that the film is preoccupied with communist invasion (30). While I agree with that metaphorical reading, following commentators like Mumford leads me to conclude that many people understood fear of communism as a displaced fear of the American (in)security state. Further, contemporary reactions to the film indicate a bifurcation in the reading of the body snatcher's metaphor. Ernesto G. Laura in a 1957 review reads the film as a simple-minded presentation of communism (71). Guy Braucourt, interviewing Siegel in 1970, views the film as a criticism of fascism. Whatever the danger is, it is the inability on the part of the citizens of Santa Mira to see the danger that the film emphasizes. Stuart Samuels notes that "Mira in Spanish means 'to look,' but the people of Santa Mira refuse to look; they stare blankly into the unknown" (209).

12. Edward Jayne makes a convincing argument that all popular fiction replicates paranoiac discourse, commenting that "the more paranoid the novel the more likely it is to enjoy widespread success" (153).

13. Peter Biskind, for example, argues that the film begins "like a radical-right film"—which is how he views *Invasion*—"but it is gradually transformed into a left-wing film as it becomes clear that the aliens mean us no harm" (149). Biskind's classification of 1950s sf films as right, center, or left, strikes me as mechanistic.

14. Several critics discuss the paranoiac's ability to decry social injustices through his or her delusory system. For example, Harold P. Blum discusses paranoia's ability to reveal social injustices (106).

15. See *The Human Radiation Experiments* for documentation of radiation experiments done on U.S. citizens in the postwar era.

Chapter 4

1. See Carol Hurd Green, Joyce Antler, and Marie Ashe.

2. Possibly the source to whom McMillan alludes is Kitty Oppenheimer. One of the issues raised in Oppenheimer's loss of his security clearance in 1954 centered on the fact that he had told his wife about the work in the laboratory. See Rachel Holloway.

3. See Bryan C. Taylor for a discussion of women in Los Alamos using reproduction as a means of combating the pressure of carrying "the secret 'inside' and 'turned inward'" ("Register" 276).

4. Interestingly, Gordon Douglas's 1954 sf film, *Them!* employs a similar metaphor for the monstrosities created by the work at Los Alamos, as I discuss in the following chapter.

5. I am using the term "feminine paranoia" to designate what I see as a particular symptomology of paranoia in women. I use the term "feminine" to indicate that this paranoia is formed in culture and hence is not "female" (that is biological) in origin.

6. See, for example, John Mirowsky and Catherine E. Ross, who discuss paranoia in Mexican-Americans. They find that "females tend to be more mistrusting and paranoid than males" (236) due to their frequent status of powerlessness within an all-too-often powerless social group. See also Christina E. Newhill for a discussion of cultural influences on paranoia. Peter K. Chadwick's study of paranoia analyzes those individuals at risk for paranoia as frequently unemployed, unhappy in their personal lives, and powerless to change their circumstances.

7. This fostering of cultural paranoia was one goal of the postwar scientists' movement. See *One World or None* for further examples.

8. Robert B. White examines Schreber's paranoia from the standpoint of Freud's theories of the pre-oedipal phase. White reads Schreber's fantasy of becoming a woman as a desire "to regress to an archaic, undifferentiated, oral-dependent fusion with her [the pre-oedipal mother]" (61).

9. Interestingly, the aliens suspend the human bodies inside the ship, attaching them to electrical wires which transmit the humans' memories and knowledge to the aliens who are posing as humans. This theory of an external-controlling machine greatly resembles Tausk's accounts of his patients' delusions about "the influencing machine."

10. I am not suggesting that either sf film is deliberately illustrating Freudian theories of paranoia. What I am suggesting is that these two films' analyses of feminine paranoia bear striking resemblances to psychoanalytic theories of paranoia. By different means, psychoanalysts and sf filmmakers make similar observations about paranoia.

11. A large majority of the over 200 nuclear atmospheric tests conducted by the United States in the postwar period were conducted in the American Southwest and West. See *The Bulletin of the Atomic Scientists* Online.

12. Christopher Guest's 1993 remake of the film domesticates the anger of Nancy Archer by making the transformation unequivocally a positive experience that results in female bonding and a newly gained sense of self-worth.

Chapter 5

1. Victorian society was dominated by a scientism that extended biological theories of evolution to the social realm. Fear of moving down the evolutionary ladder instead of up it predominated in social theories especially toward the end of the nineteenth-century. Imaginative works such as Robert Louis Stevenson's *The Strange Case of Doctor Jekyll and Mr. Hyde* and H. G. Wells' *The Island of Doctor Moreau* attest to the fear of human society becoming more animalistic. See the collection of essays *Degeneration: The Dark Side of Progress,* eds. Edward J. Chamberlin and Sander L. Gilman.

2. Frederick Pohl's *The Midas Plague* (1954) comically portrays a future in which atomic power has created a leisure society so economically and materially abundant that conspicuous consumption becomes a duty placed on each American citizen.

3. A letter written to *Time* in 1945 compares the use of the atomic bomb on Japan as worse than Nazi war crimes and calls the bomb "this Frankenstein monster." A 1946 article in *Time* entitled "The Broken Mirror" refers to the bomb as "The Thing" (29). See also Paul Boyer and Spencer Weart for further discussions of the bomb as Frankenstein monster and mythological Thing.

4. Genesis references abound in early discussions of the bomb. See, for example, Laurence, whose tour of the Oak Ridge plant makes him remark that the plant produces elements akin to the creation present in Genesis (163).

5. This conflation also displaces the affect of the Bomb onto a prehistory, thus making it outside of time and somehow universal. See Chapter 7 for further discussion of this idea.

6. Susan Sontag's influential essay "The Imagination of Disaster" sees this displacement of real nuclear war onto fantastic monsters as essentially an escapist one. My view, however, is that because nuclear war is the unrepresentable, the unthinkable, metaphors are the only way to powerfully capture meaning when dealing with the bomb. See Jacques Derrida's essay "No Apocalypse, Not Now (full speed ahead, seven missiles, seven missives)."

7. Andrew Tudor argues that 1950s horror is characterized by perception of scientists "*unwittingly* causing disaster" as opposed to the deliberately malicious scientists who pervaded 1930s horror films (134).

8. See David Bradley's account of the Bikini test, *No Place to Hide* (1948), in which he discusses radiation sickness as being associated with "the terrors of the supernatural" (153). For a specific discussion of the beast as metaphor see Vivian Sobchack who discusses the creature as both primeval force and new atomic force ("Virginity" 111).

9. In Schreber's *Memoirs,* he portrays himself as both the cause of the apocalyptic destruction of the world, which takes place in his delusion and the solution, and as the savior who will build a new world. The scientists' movement displays a similar paranoiac logic: the scientists who created the bomb attempting to save the world from its consequences. See Chapter 2 of this study.

10. A source for *Beast,* Ray Bradbury's short story "The Foghorn" (1951) portrays the beast as a tragic figure, one whose primeval instincts are juxtaposed with a war-torn and alienating modern world. One character in the story comments apropos of the beast, "while we've paraded around with trumpets, lopping off each other's countries and heads, they have been living beneath the sea twelve miles deep and cold in a time as old as the beard of a comet" (2).

11. Harry and Bonaro Overstreet also comment on the facade of progression supposedly used by communists, arguing that in 1935 the American communist party "began to call itself a 'progressive' American party" (7-8).

12. Delusions involving insects or insectlike creatures pervade paranoia. Schreber hallucinated God placing scorpions in his head. Ronald K. Siegel discusses several paranoiac patients who have insect delusions, including one man who believes that insects have been injected into his body and are eating his brain.

13. See Boyer and Weart for discussions of ways in which the Atoms for Peace program promoted the benefits of radiation treatment for disease.

14. Vivian Sobchack notes that both the destroyed trailer at the beginning of the film and Gramps' store point to "a process of erosion which will eat away all traces of Man" (*Screening* 116-17).

15. See Bryan C. Taylor for a discussion of "atomized workers" at Los Alamos who were organized "to participate in a rationally biased commitment to technological innovation" (*"Reminiscences"* 433). Nora Sayre notes that the emphasis the film puts on the social organization of the ants "sounds like a Bolshevik trait" (193).

16. Peter Biskind argues, for example, that the film is a conservative "attack on women in a man's world" (133). Mark Jancovich takes up the same sort of localized reading of the film, arguing contra Biskind that the film portrays Pat Medford as a positive female authority figure. Jancovich believes that the queens' gender is irrelevant to the film's portrayal of totalitarianism and conformity, a view with which I clearly disagree. Michael Rogin argues that *Them!* joins "nature's revenge against man to the triumph of mass society" (29). His article argues that frequently lurking beneath Cold War films' suspicion of communism is a suspicion of the mother.

17. See Kathyrn Hume for a discussion of degeneration theory in Wells' *The Time Machine.* Hume relates the novel to Victorian Darwinian and entropic theories of devolution.

18. See Brian Easlea and Evelyn Fox Keller for analyses of the modern world's gendering of scientific progress as masculine and chaotic nature as feminine.

19. A review of the film in *Catholic World* recommends that *"Them!* certainly isn't for softies" (144). Arthur Knight feels less than reassured that the growth of the ants is scientifically impossible, commenting, "At least, that's what the experts tell me" (27). Moira Walsh shares Knight's fear, stating that "it is my sincere and fairly assured hope that this premise is preposterous" (367). *The Commonweal* review of the film argues that it sends the audience away "with some somber food for thought" (270).

20. For other discussions of masculinity in the novel and film, see Paul Wells who traces Scott's loss of masculinity in the film, concluding that Scott is being punished for "the sin of patriarchy in its oppression and devaluation of women" (192). I do not read the film as having a feminist agenda, as does Wells, but, rather as highlighting the breakdown of traditional gender roles as one of the problems of the Atomic Age. Adam Knee views the film as a "lurid dramatization of fifties white patriarchal power and culture under siege" (31). In my view the film is an expose of the insecurities plaguing the supposedly secure, confidant 1950s white male. Margaret Tarratt views Scott as immersed in a world dominated by "fear of castration by the female" (27). Tarratt sees Scott's battle with the cat and spider as displaced conflicts with Louise. I see the gendering of the basement on a more global level of civilization versus devolution. See also Jancovich, who examines Scott's anxieties about his masculine role in relation to a 1950s corporate ideal of manliness.

21. In Matheson's novel, Scott literally becomes a toy for his daughter, Beth.

22. Arnold's film changes the spider from a black widow to a tarantula, but the association of the basement with a feminine space is maintained.

23. See Ilya Prigogine and Isabelle Stengers for a discussion of contemporary science's movement away from a conception of the universe as a closed system, a view which has been held by modern science from Newton through the twentieth century.

Chapter 6

1. See Jim Holte for a discussion of Puritanism as a defining feature of sf. Holte argues, "The Puritan may have traded in his steeple hat and black coat for a space helmet and thruster pack, but he is still dedicated to continuing the heroic quest and to avoiding or sublimating all serious sexual expression in the process" (184). See also Albert I. Berger, who examines sexual displacement in sf ("Love"). Vivian Sobchack's discussion of sex and sf film is a strong one. Sobchack argues that "More than any other American film genre, then, science fiction denies human eroticism and libido a traditional narrative representation

and expression" ("Virginity"103). While Sobchack views the monsters of sf as embodying female sexuality, I would extend this formulation to include sexuality *per se* in 1950s sf films. Margaret Tarratt argues that the creatures in 1950s sf films speak to the disjunction between "publicly accepted social sexual mores and the actual sexual needs of the individual" (269). Russian sf writer Stanislaw Lem comments that "all sf suffers in the realm of 'cosmic sexual life' from Victorianism and puritanism (which are inborn sicknesses that result in a paralysis of thought and imagination)" (314-15).

2. Hayworth was horrified that her picture appeared on the bomb shell. See Barbara Leaming. Testimony of those growing up during the postwar period points to the fact that they frequently associated nuclear war with sexual thrill. In Martin Wangh's study of psychoanalysts who grew up in the 1950s, he relates that one man "remembers reading the book 'On The Beach' for sexual content . . . The 'world' was going to end so they threw away all caution'": a woman then comments that "Other girls read it, but I think they were also only interested in sex" (ellipsis in original; 315-316). Other examples include a teenage girl on *The Honeymooners* who referred to her boyfriend as "Atomic Passion," and a publicity stunt for the sale of bomb shelters which had a honeymoon couple spend two weeks in a shelter, the result of which was that the couple received a trip to Mexico (Miller and Nowak 47; 51-52). See Elaine Tyler May for further discussion of the linking of female sexuality and the bomb in postwar culture.

3. See A. Constandina Titus and Jerry L. Simich for a more thorough discussion of atomic music. They examine the 1950s split between moralizing country-and-western songs about the Bomb and erotic rock-and-roll songs about it.

4. See Paul Boyer and Spencer Weart for further examples of sexualization of the Bomb in the 1940s and 1950s. Weart notes that postwar journalists believed that "the press treated atomic energy in the cramped way they had once talked about sex" (125).

6. For example, Stanley Bone and John M. Oldham see Schreber's paranoia as stemming from gender uncertainty: "For Freud, behaviors that today could be labeled as culturally 'feminine' would have been labeled as typically homosexual in males" (7). To a certain extent, 1950s culture still held the notion that lack of clear gender identification equaled homosexuality. See, for example, Barbara Ehrenreich.

7. See William G. Niederland, Robert B. White, Janine Chasseguet-Smirgel, and Eric L. Santer for discussions of Schreber along these alternative lines.

8. See also Victor Tausk, who discusses paranoiac patients who believed that their energy was being drained by "influencing machines," which often manipulated them sexually. Peter R. Chadwick comments on a paranoiac who

believed "women were coming into his room while he was asleep and having intercourse with him while his penis was erect during REM (rapid eye movement) sleep" (22).

9. See Norman Cameron, for a discussion of paranoiac delusion beginning on the sexual level because of the disjunction between the privacy of sexuality and the social world mature men and women must function within.

10. For another example of the perception of the bomb as supernatural force, see David Bradley's account of the Bikini Test in *No Place to Hide*.

11. Frank D. McConnell comments on the battle between David and Mark being an attempt to define "what sort of 'manhood' their culture will tolerate or sanction" (22)

12. Other 1950s sf films which deal with evolutionary themes include *Them!*, *The Beast from 20,000 Fathoms*, *The Incredible Shrinking Man*, *It Came from Outer Space*, *The Deadly Mantis*, and *Tarantula*. See Chapter 5 of this book.

13. Weart notes that "a psychological survey of young people in the mid-1960s confirmed that in their thoughts of imminent nuclear bombing, reality was reinforcing adolescent fantasies about inadequate and destructive adults" (340).

14. McConnell comments apropos of the first creature film that the creature functions less as a symbol and more as a hieroglyph, "an icon for the infinitely variable but single-minded urging of the libido" (20). I agree, and believe that it is the inability to associate the creature as sexuality on a one-to-one basis with a single character in either film that gives the creature the metaphorical power that he possesses. John Baxter discusses the creature being "other-directed," as part of a world "where our ideas of morality have no relevance" (121). While I agree that the creature is being portrayed as other from human men, he does, however, possess a chivalric code of behavior that is clearly part of human conceptions of honor.

15.The third gill-man film is *The Creature Walks Among Us* (1956), directed by John Sherwood. I do not discuss this film because I do not perceive there the complex intertwining between nuclear fear and desire I discern in the two Arnold films. The evolutionary theme is present, as the creature is literally becoming an air-breathing man in the film, but the association of the creature with sexuality is minimal.

Chapter 7

1. *Time* magazine's initial response to the bomb also used the Prometheus analogy. Discussing the progress believed to be inherent in the bomb, *Time* comments, "a dim folk memory had preserved the story of a greater advance: 'the winged hound of Zeus' tearing from Prometheus' liver the price of fire" ("U.S." 29).

2. Lacan's conception of the Real helps to articulate trauma. For Lacan, the Real represents the attempt on the part of pre-imaginary reality to speak. Since signification cuts us off from reality, the Real speaks only in gaps, only by frustrating the Symbolic. The Real of Hiroshima and Nagasaki can never be directly symbolized or spoken. Frederic Jameson uses the concept of the Real to articulate a theory of history in *The Political Unconscious*. Jameson argues that "History is what hurts," but it can be expressed and understood "only through its effects, and never directly as some reified force" (102).

3. Bataille wrote this article in 1947. Current estimates place the death rate at 100,000 and the fatal injury rate at 50,000 (Lifton and Mitchell xvii). The realization that human agency can be responsible for total death defies the imagination. Leo Botstein argues that effectively conceptualizing nuclear war may be impossible: "Total death cannot truly even be imagined; no myth appeared even necessary for Freud. One may, in fact, not be able to create effective psychological myths for the unimaginable prospect which has, only since nuclear weapons, become part of reality, both external and psychological" (301). Botstein, like Bataille, also relates the horror of nuclear weapons to the fact that "that annihilation can occur by our own actions" (304). The technique of mythologizing the bomb may come from any point on the political spectrum. John Berger's essay "Hiroshima," for example, deplores the bombings of Hiroshima as terrorist acts, yet in his interpretation of survivors' paintings, he ultimately concludes that they are paintings of hell. Berger argues that "nobody can confront the reality of 6th August 1945 without being forced to acknowledge that what happened was evil" (581). Viewing the bombing of Hiroshima as an act of evil removes it from historical time.

4. Psychoanalysis itself is often accused of committing the same delusory work of removing history from the individual and vice versa. See John Farrell, for a placing of psychoanalysis within the context of modern paranoia. See the collection *Psychoanalysis and the Nuclear Threat* (eds. Levine, Jacobs, and Rubin) for a collection of psychoanalytic articles that address the specific historical circumstances of nuclear society.

5. See Eric L. Santner's fine study *My Own Private Germany* for further discussion of the cultural events present in Schreber's delusory system. In his introduction to the book Santner links the current academic interest in paranoia to a reflection on/desire for the Cold War: "Nostalgia for the more ordered world of cold war anxieties would appear to be a nostalgia for a paranoia in which the persecutor had a more or less recognizable face and a clear geographic location" (xiii-xiv).

6. There are abundant postwar references to the Soviets as mythologically evil. The Soviet Union is routinely associated with Ancient Rome and Ancient Egypt (De Mille's *The Ten Commandments* [1956] is a good example). See Nora Sayre for further discussion of Rome and Egypt as vehicles for allegoriz-

ing the Soviet Union. During 1949 Attorney General Howard McGrath called various groups to arms in the "modern struggle against pagan communist philosophies that seek to enslave the world" (qtd. in Wittner 86). Hanna M. Segal argues that in the paranoiac Cold War mentality "to hide our own aggressive desires, we have to project the evil onto an enemy—real or imaginary—he must appear to be an inhuman monster" (39).

7. Another way to theorize this view of the Soviet Union is that it served as the *objet petit a* for American society during the Cold War. Lacan comments that the *objet a* is "the object that cannot be swallowed, as it were, which remains stuck in the gullet of the signifier" (*Four* 270). As Parveen Adams comments apropos of *jouissance,* "it is the real, that which Lacan famously announced is impossible. But that does not mean it is irrelevant. It irrupts and disturbs the life of the symbolic order. That which comes to the symbolic from the real, Lacan calls the *objet petit a*" (186). The *objet a* is a fantasy object which attempts to fill up lack in the symbolic. As a fantasy object, it questions and threatens the ideological as reality. Stone humorously deflates the fantasy power of the Soviet Union by pondering how communist teachers always brainwash their students: "How do they do it in Latin? By blaming the conjunctions on capitalism? Or geology? By hinting that rocks are bigger in the Soviet Union?" (178).

8. Richard Hodgens levels this type of criticism especially at sf films which, he claims, associate technology with "The Black Arts" (261). Frederic Jameson argues that sf attests to the inability of capitalist society to imagine the future. He argues that sf's "deepest vocation is over and over again to demonstrate and to dramatize our incapacity to imagine the future" ("Progress" 153).

9. See my "Paranoia and the Delusion of the Total System" for further discussion of connections between paranoia and the prevalence of scientific discourse in modern society.

10. Brands argues that implications of the atomic bomb hit the United States particularly hard because "few peoples have placed such store in the future as Americans, for whom each generation promised, and usually delivered, greater wealth and power than the previous generation" (67-68).

11. Gianni Vattimo argues apropos of postmodern notions of an end to history that only continued belief in a positivist system refuses to accept facts like Stalinism and Nazism as part of the process of history (135).

12. Harry Truman himself possessed a static view of history that caused him to comment, "There's nothing new in human nature; only our names for things change. Read the lives of Roman emperors from Claudius to Constantine if you want some inside dope on the 20th century . . ." (qtd. in Lifton and Mitchell 195).

13. Benjamin Shapiro argues that sf's generic construction works to assimilate new historical events into mythic continuity: "How can there even be any

sense of continuous time and universal truths? The answer lies in the linking of mythic past with the historical, experienced present and the hopeful projection of contemporary values and paradigms into the terrifying, unimaginable future" (104).

14. The phenomenon "was large drops of moisture formed by minute particles of carbon thrown up by the heat, forming water vapour when it reached layers of cold air. These became charged with radioactive dust and fell in isolated showers of what everyone referred to as 'black rain'" (Burchett 66).

Chapter 8

1. Paul Boyer argues that "Having accepted terror bombing as essential to the nation's purposes, most Americans seem to have viewed the atomic bomb as a fearsome but ethically indistinguishable technical means to a legitimate strategic purpose" (215).

2. John H. Dower relates that survivors of the atomic bombs suffer "higher-than-normal rates of leukemia and cancers of the thyroid, breast, lung, stomach, and salivary glands." He also notes that many unborn infants exposed to the bombs were born mentally retarded and have been mentally disabled now for fifty years.

3. In a 1960 interview, Manhattan Project scientist Leo Szilard, an open opponent of the use of the atomic bomb, maintains that Truman did not understand the magnitude of the bomb. He argues that "Truman did not understand what was involved. You can see that from the language he used . . . to put the atomic bomb in terms of having gambled 2 billion dollars and having 'won' offended my sense of proportion, and I concluded at the time that Truman did not understand at all what was involved" ("President" 70). If Szilard's observations are correct, Truman did, however, have a sense of the horrible new power of the bomb. Even if he publicly portrayed it as merely another military device, privately he was haunted by its incredible destructive power.

4. Hersey's account was immediately criticized for minimizing the radical nature of the attack. Both Mary McCarthy and Dwight MacDonald savaged Hersey's approach to the catastrophe. See Lifton and Mitchell (88-89) and Yavenditti (41).

5. See Michael J. Yavenditti for further discussion of De Seversky's article as a counter to Hersey's *Hiroshima*.

6. See Boyer (325-26) for detailed discussion of these articles and others dealing with the survivability of nuclear war.

7. See Gar Alperovitz and Lifton and Mitchell for discussions of the circumstances under which Stimson's name was attached to this article.

8. Hollywood's first representation of the bomb, *The Beginning or the End,* portrays planes for ten days dropping leaflets on Hiroshima warning of the impending attack.

9. The notion of God intervening to save the earth is the biggest departure from Wells' novel that the film makes. In Wells' novel, the curate is portrayed as irrational and weak. Wells' narrator responds to the curate's view that God is punishing the earth through the invasion by stating, "The tremendous tragedy in which he had been involved—it was evident he was a fugitive from Weybridge—had driven him to the very verge of his reason" (108-09). Robert Torry argues that the divine intervention in the film makes "nuclear weapons irrelevant to a divinely sanctioned defeat of the godless by the faithful" (19). See also Roger A. Berger for a discussion of Wells' novels within the context of Cold War films.

WORKS CITED

Adams, Henry. "A Letter to American Teachers of History." 1910. *The Degradation of the Democratic Dogma*. New York: Macmillan, 1920.

Adams, Parveen. "Father, Can't You See I'm Filming?" *Supposing the Subject*. Ed. Joan Copjec. London: Verso, 1994. 185-200.

Alexander, Franz. "Adventure and Security in a Changing World." 1957. *The Scope of Psychoanalysis 1921-1961: Selected Papers of Franz Alexander*. New York: Basic, 1961. 462-72.

Allen, Raymond B. "Communists Should Not Teach in American Colleges." *Educational Forum* 13.4 (May 1949): 1-7.

Allison, David B, et al., eds. *Psychosis and Sexual Identity: Toward a Post-Analytic View of the Schreber Case*. Albany: SUNY UP, 1988.

Alperovitz, Gar. *The Decision to Use the Atomic Bomb and the Architecture of an American Myth*. New York: Knopf, 1995.

Alsop, Joseph, and Stewart Alsop. "Your Flesh Should Creep." *Saturday Evening Post* 13 July 1946: 9, 49-50.

"Anatomic Bomb." *Life* 3 Sept. 1945: 53-54.

Antler, Joyce. "A Bond of Sisterhood: Ethel Rosenberg, Molly Goldberg, and Radical Jewish Women of the 1950s." *Secret Agents*. Eds. Garber and Walkowitz. 197-214.

Ashe, Marie. "*The Bell Jar* and the Ghost of Ethel Rosenberg." *Secret Agents*. Eds. Garber and Walkowitz. 215-31.

"The Atomic Bombings of Hiroshima and Nagasaki by the Manhattan Engineering District, June 29, 1946." Trinity Atomic Web Site. Online. Available: <http://www.environlist.org>.

Attack of the 50 Ft. Woman. Dir. Nathan Juran. Allied Artists, 1958.

Auchincloss, Elizabeth L., and Richard W. Weiss. "Paranoid Character and the Intolerance of Indifference." *Paranoia: New Psychoanalytic Perspectives*. Eds. Stanley Oldham and Stanley Bone. 27-48.

Badash, Lawrence. Introduction. *Reminiscences of Los Alamos*. Eds. Badash, Hirshfelder, and Broida. xi-xxi.

Badash, Lawrence, Joseph O. Hirshfelder, and Herbert P. Broida, eds. *Reminiscences of Los Alamos 1943-1945*. Boston: Reidel, 1980.

Barson, Michael. *'Better Dead Than Red': A Nostalgic Look at the Golden Years of RussiaPhobia, Red-Baiting, and Other Commie Madness*. New York: Hyperion, 1992.

Bartter, Martha A. *The Way to Ground Zero: The Atomic Bomb in American Science Fiction.* New York: Greenwood P, 1988.

Bataille, George. "Concerning the Accounts Given by the Residents of Hiroshima." Trans. Alan Keenen. *Trauma: Explorations in Memory.* Ed. Cathy Caruth. 21-35.

Bates, Harry. "Farewell to the Master." *Reel Future.* 1940. Eds. Forrest J. Ackerman and Jean Stine. New York: Barnes and Noble, 1994. 146-79.

Baxter, John. *Science Fiction in the Cinema.* New York: Barnes, 1970.

The Beast from 20,000 Fathoms. Dir. Eugene Lourie. Warner Brothers, 1953.

Berger, Albert I. "Love, Death, and the Atomic Bomb: Sexuality and Community in Science Fiction, 1935-55." *Science-Fiction Studies* 8.3 (Nov. 1981): 280-96.

——. "The Triumph of Prophesy: Science Fiction and Nuclear Power in the Post-Hiroshima Period." *Science-Fiction Studies* 3.2 (July 1976): 143-50.

Berger, John. "Hiroshima." *Fields of Writing: Readings Across the Disciplines.* 1981. 4th ed. Eds. Nancy Comley, et al. New York: St. Martin's, 1994. 575-82.

Berger, Roger A. " 'Ask What You Can Do for Your Country': The Film Version of H. G. Wells's *The Time Machine* and The Cold War." *Literature/Film Quarterly* 17.3 (1989): 177-87.

Bernbabeu, Edith P. "Science Fiction: A New Mythos." *Psychoanalytical Quarterly* 26 (Oct. 1957): 527-35.

Biskind, Peter. *Seeing Is Believing: How Hollywood Taught Us to Stop Worrying and Love the Fifties.* New York: Pantheon, 1983.

Blum, Harold P. "Paranoid Betrayal and Jealousy: The Loss and Restitution of Object Constancy." *Paranoia.* Eds. Oldham and Bone. 97-114.

Bohr, Niels. "Forward: Science and Civilization." *One World or None.* Eds. Masters and Way. ix-x.

Bone, Stanley, and John M. Oldham. "Paranoia: Historical Considerations." *Paranoia: New Psychoanalytic Perspectives.* Eds. Oldham and Bone. 3-15.

Botstein, Leon. "Freud on War and Death: Thoughts from a Nuclear Perspective." *Psychoanalysis and Contemporary Thought* 7 (1984): 291-338.

Boyarin, Daniel. "Freud's Baby, Fliess's Maybe: Homophobia, Anti-Semitism, and the Invention of Oedipus." *GLQ* 2 (1995): 115-47.

Boyer, Paul. *By the Bomb's Early Light: American Thought and Culture at the Dawn of the Atomic Age.* New York: Pantheon, 1985.

Bradbury, Ray. "The Foghorn." *The Golden Apples of the Sun.* 1951. New York: Bantam, 1961.

Bradley, David. *No Place to Hide.* 1948. Hanover, NH: UP of New England, 1983.

Brands, H. W. *The Devil We Knew: Americans and the Cold War.* New York: Oxford UP, 1993.

Braucort, Guy. "Interview with Don Siegel." *Focus on the Science Fiction Film.* Ed. William Johnson. Englewood Cliffs, NJ: Prentice-Hall, 1972. 74-76.

Brode, Bernice. "Tales of Los Alamos." *Reminiscences of Los Alamos.* Eds. Badash, Hirschfelder, and Broida. 133-59.

"The Broken Mirror." *Time* 15 July 1946: 28-29.

Brosnan, John. *Future Tense: The Cinema of Science Fiction.* New York: St. Martin's, 1978.

Brown, Harrison. *Must Destruction Be Our Destiny?* New York: Simon and Schuster, 1946.

The Bulletin of the Atomic Scientists. Online. 26 July 1996. Available: http://wwwbull atomsci.org

Burgess, Ernest W., and Paul Wallin. *Engagement and Marriage.* Chicago: Lippincott, 1953.

Cameron, N. "The Paranoid Pseudo-Community." *American Journal of Sociology* 49 (1943): 32-38.

——. "The Paranoid Pseudo-Community Revisited." *American Journal of Sociology* 64 (1959): 52-58.

Caruth, Cathy. "An Interview with Robert Jay Lifton." *Trauma: Explorations in Memory.* Ed. Caruth. 128-47.

——. Introduction. *Trauma: Explorations in Memory.* 151-57.

Caruth, Cathy, ed. *Trauma: Explorations in Memory.* Baltimore: Johns Hopkins UP, 1995.

Chadwick, Peter K. *Borderline: A Psychological Study of Paranoia and Delusional Thinking.* New York: Routledge, 1992.

Chamberlin, J. Edward, and Sander L. Gilman, eds. *Degeneration: The Dark Side of Progress.* New York: Columbia UP, 1985.

Chasseguet-Smirgel, Janine. "On President Schreber's Transsexual Delusion." *Psychosis and Sexual Identity: Toward a Post-Analytic View of the Schreber Case.* Eds. David B. Allison, et al. 155-68.

Compton, Arthur. Introduction. *One World or None.* Eds. Masters and Way. v-vi.

——. "Now That We've Burst the Atom." *Rotarian* 9 Oct. 1945: 8-9.

Compton, Karl T. "If the Atomic Bomb Had Not Been Used." *Atlantic Monthly* July-Dec. 1946: 54-56.

Condon, E. U. "The New Technique of Private War." *One World or None.* Eds. Masters and Way. 39-41.

Conners, Leila. "Present at the Detonation." *New Perspectives Quarterly* 12 (1995): 43-45.

Copjec, Joan. "The Anxiety of the Influencing Machine." *October* 23 (Winter 1982): 43-59.

Copjec, Joan, ed. *Shades of Noir: A Reader.* London: Verso, 1993.

Corner, George M. *Attaining Manhood: A Doctor Talks to Boys About Sex.* 2nd ed. New York: Harper and Row, 1952.

Creature from the Black Lagoon. Dir. Jack Arnold. Universal, 1954.

The Day the Earth Stood Still. Dir. Robert Wise. Twentieth-Century Fox, 1951.

"A Decision for Mankind." *St. Louis Post-Dispatch* 7 Aug. 1945.

De Oliveira, Prado. "Schreber, Ladies and Gentlemen." *Psychosis and Sexual Identity: Towards a Post-Analytic View of the Schreber Case*. Eds. David B. Allison, et al. 169-79.

Derrida, Jacques. "No Apocalypse, Not Now (full speed ahead, seven missiles, seven missives)." Trans. Catherine Porter and Philip Lewis. *Diacritics* 14.2 (Summer 1984): 20-31.

de Seversky, Major Alexander P. "Atomic Bomb Hysteria." *Reader's Digest* Jan. 1946: 121-26.

Dower, John W. "Hiroshima, Nagasaki, and The Politics of Memory." *Technology Review* Aug/Sept. 1995. Online. Available: http://www.mit.edu

Dowling, D. H. "The Atomic Scientist: Machine or Moralist?" *Science-Fiction Studies* 13.2 (July 1986): 139-47.

Durgnat, Raymond. *Films and Feelings*. Cambridge, MA: MIT P, 1967.

Earth Vs. the Flying Saucers. Dir. Fred F. Sears. Columbia, 1956.

"*Earth Vs. the Flying Saucers*." *BoxOffice*. 2 June 1956. Online. Available: http://www.boxoffice.com.

Easlea, Brian. *Fathering the Unthinkable: Masculinity, Scientists and the Nuclear Arms Race*. London: Pluto P, 1983.

Ehrenreich, Barbara. *The Hearts of Men: American Dreams and the Flight from Commitment*. New York: Doubleday, 1983.

Einstein, Albert. "Einstein on the Atomic Bomb." *The Atlantic Monthly* Nov. 1945: 43-45.

——. "The Way Out." *One World or None*. Eds. Masters and Way. 76-77.

Ellegard, Alvar. *Darwin and the General Reader*. 1958. Chicago: U of Chicago P, 1990.

Ellis, Albert. *The American Sexual Tragedy*. New York: Twayne, 1954.

Enriquez, Micheline. "Paranoiac Fantasies: Sexual Difference, Homosexuality, Law of the Father." *Psychosis*. Ed. Allison, et al. 102-29.

Farrell, John. *Freud's Paranoid Quest: Psychoanalysis and Modern Suspicion*. New York: New York UP, 1996.

Ferenczi, Sandor. *Sex in Psychoanalysis*. 1912. Trans. Ernest Jones. New York: Basic, 1950.

Fermi, Laura. *Atoms in the Family: My Life with Enrico Fermi*. 1954. Chicago: U of Chicago P, 1995.

——. "The Fermis' Path to Los Alamos." *Reminiscences of Los Alamos*. Eds. Badash, Hirschfelder, and, Broida. 89-103.

Ferrell, Robert H. *Off The Record: The Private Papers of Harry S. Truman*. New York: Harper and Row, 1980.

Feynman, Richard P. "Los Alamos from Below." *Reminiscences of Los Alamos.* Eds. Badash, Hirshfelder, and Broida. 105-32.

Filreis, Alan. "'Words with All the Effects of Force': Cold War Interpretation." *American Quarterly* 39 (Summer 1987): 306-12.

Finney, Jack. *The Body Snatchers.* New York: Dell, 1955.

Folson, Joseph K. "Steps in Love and Courtship." *Family, Marriage and Parenthood.* 2nd ed. Eds. Howard Becker and Reuben Hill. Boston: Heath, 1955. 205-45.

Franklin, H. Bruce. *War Stars: The Superweapon and the American Imagination.* New York: Oxford UP, 1988.

Freedman, Carl. "Towards a Theory of Paranoia: The Science Fiction of Philip K. Dick." *Science-Fiction Studies* 11 (1984): 15-24.

Freeman, Barbara. "Epitaphs and Epigraphs: 'The End(s) of Man.'" *Arms and the Woman: War, Gender, and Literary Representations.* Eds. Helen M. Cooper, et al. Chapel Hill: U of North Carolina P, 1989. 303-22.

Freeman, Carl. "Towards an Theory of Paranoia: The Science Fiction of Philip K. Dick." *Science-Fiction Studies* 11 (1984): 15-24.

Freud, Sigmund. "A Case of Paranoia Running Counter to the Psychoanalytic Theory of the Disease." *The Standard Edition of the Complete Psychological Works of Sigmund Freud.* Vol. 14. 1915. Trans. and ed. James Strachey. London: Hogarth, 1957. 263-72.

——. "Further Remarks on the Neuro-Psychoses of Defence." *Standard Edition* 2 (1896): 162-85.

——. "Mourning and Melancholia." *Standard Edition* 14 (1917): 239-60.

——. "Psychoanalytic Notes Upon an Autobiographical Account of a Case of Paranoia (Dementia Paranoides)." *Three Case Histories.* 1911. Ed. Philip Rieff. New York: Collier, 1963.

——. "The Psychology of Women, Lecture XXXIII." *New Introductory Lectures on Psychoanalysis.* Trans. W. J. H. Sprott. New York: Norton, 1933. 153-85.

Gabbard, Krin. "Religious and Political Allegory in Robert Wise's *The Day the Earth Stood Still.*" *Literature/Film Quarterly* 10.3 (1982): 150-54.

Garber, Marjorie, and Rebecca L. Walkowitz, eds. *Secret Agents: The Rosenberg Case, McCarthyism, and Fifties America.* New York: Routledge, 1995.

Geller, Jay. "Freud vs. Freud: Freud's Readings of Daniel Paul Schreber's *Denkwürdigkeiten eines Nervenkranken.*" *Reading Freud's Reading.* Eds. Sander L. Gilman, et al. New York: New York UP, 1994. 243-82.

Gifford, Sanford. "Freud's Fearful Symmetry: Further Reflections on the Life and Death Instincts." *Psychoanalysis and the Nuclear Threat.* Eds. Levine, Jacobs, and Rubin. 15-34.

"Global Nuclear Stockpiles, 1945-1997." *The Bulletin of the Atomic Scientists* Nov.-Dec. 1997: 67.

Goldburg, Stanley. "The Secret About Secrets." *Secret Agents*. Eds. Garber and Walkowitz. 47-58.

Goldwert, Marvin. "Teleology and Paranoia: The Search for Meaning." *Psychological Reports* 72 (1993): 326.

Grant, Barry K. "Invaders from Mars and the Science Fiction Film in the Age of Reagan." *Cineaction!* 8 (1987): 77-83.

Green, Carol Hurd. "The Suffering Body: Ethel Rosenberg in the Hands of the Writers." *Secret Agents*. Eds. Garber and Walkowitz. 183-95.

Groves, Gen. L. R. "Memorandum for the Secretary of War." Trinity Atomic Web Site. Online. Available: <http://www.environlist.org>.

Gruman, Harris L. "Freud's 'Forgetting of Foreign Words': The History of the Jews between Parody and Paranoia." *History and Memory* 6.2 (1994): 125-51.

Halberstam, David. *The Fifties*. New York: Villard, 1993.

Hendershot, Cyndy. "Paranoia and the Delusion of the Total System." *American Imago* 54.1 (Spring 1997): 15-37.

——. "Vampire and Replicant: The One-Sex Body in a Two-Sex World." *Science-Fiction Studies* 22.3 (Nov. 1995): 373-98.

Hersey, John. *Hiroshima*. 1946. New York: Vintage, 1989.

Hillegas, Mark R. "Science Fiction as Cultural Phenomenon: A Re-Evaluation." 1963. *SF: The Other Side of Realism: Essays on Modern Fantasy and Science Fiction*. Ed. Thomas D. Clareson. Bowling Green, OH: Bowling Green State University Popular Press, 1971. 272-81.

Hirshfelder, Joseph O. "The Scientific and Technological Miracle at Los Alamos." *Reminiscences of Los Alamos*. Eds. Badash, Hirshfelder, and Broida. 67-88.

Hoberman, J. "Paranoia and the Pod People." *Sight and Sound* 4.5 (May 1994): 28-31.

Hodgens, Richard. "A Short Tragical History of the Science Fiction Film." 1959. *SF: The Other Side of Realism: Essays on Modern Fantasy and Science Fiction*. Ed. Thomas D. Clareson. Bowling Green, OH: Bowling Green State University Popular Press, 1971. 248-62.

Hofstadter, Richard. "The Paranoid Style in American Politics." *The Paranoid Style in American Politics and Other Essays*. New York: Knopf, 1966. 3-40.

Holloway, Rachel. *In the Matter of J. Robert Oppenheimer: Politics, Rhetoric, and Self-Defense*. Westport, CT: Praeger, 1993.

Holte, Jim. "Pilgrims in Space: Puritan Ideology and the American Science Fiction Film." *Eros in the Mind's Eye: Sexuality and the Fantastic in Art and Film*. Ed. Donald Palumbo. New York: Greenwood P, 1986. 181-92.

The Human Radiation Experiments: Final Report of the Advisory Committee on Human Radiation Experiments. New York: Oxford UP, 1996.

Hume, Kathryn. "Eat or Be Eaten: H. G. Wells's *The Time Machine.*" *Philological Quarterly* 69.2 (Spring 1990): 233-51.

I Married a Monster from Outer Space. Dir. Gene Fowler. Paramount, 1958.

The Incredible Shrinking Man. Dir. Jack Arnold. Universal, 1957.

"Interview with Edward Teller." Lawrence Livermore National Laboratory. Online. 2 June 1996. Available: http://www.llnl.gov

Invaders from Mars. Dir. William Cameron Menzies. 20th Century-Fox, 1953.

Invasion of the Body Snatchers. Dir. Don Siegel. Allied Artists, 1956.

Invasion USA. Dir. Alfred E. Green. 1952.

Irigaray, Luce. "Is the Subject of Science Sexed?" Trans. Edith Oberle. *Cultural Critique* 1 (1985): 73-88.

It Came from Outer Space. Dir. Jack Arnold. Universal, 1953.

Jameson, Frederic. *The Political Unconscious: Narrative as a Socially Symbolic Act.* Ithaca: Cornell UP, 1981.

——. "Progress Versus Utopia; Or, Can We Imagine the Future?" *Science-Fiction Studies* 9 (1982): 147-58.

Jancovich, Mark. *Rational Fears: American Horror in the 1950s.* Manchester: Manchester UP, 1996.

Jayne, Edward. "The Dialectics of Paranoid Form." *Genre* 2 (1978): 131-57.

Jette, Eleanor. *Inside Box 1663.* Los Alamos, NM: Los Alamos Historical Society, 1977.

Jones, Raymond F. *This Island Earth. Reel Future.* 1952. Eds. Forrest J. Ackerman and Jean Stine. New York: Barnes and Noble, 1994. 180-299.

Kaplan, E. Ann, ed. *Women in Film Noir.* London: BFI, 1978.

Katan, M. "Schreber's Prepsychotic Phase." *The International Journal of Psychoanalysis* 34 (1953): 43-51.

Keller, Evelyn Fox. *Reflections on Gender and Science.* New Haven: Yale UP, 1985.

Killers from Space. Dir. W. Lee Wilder. RKO, 1954.

King, L. D. P. "The Development of Nuclear Explosives and Frontier Days at Los Alamos." *Behind Tall Fences: Stories and Experiences About Los Alamos at Its Beginning.* Los Alamos, NM: Los Alamos Historical Society, 1996. 57-68.

Kistiakowsky, George B. "Reminiscences of Wartime Los Alamos." *Reminiscences of Los Alamos.* Eds. Badash, Hirschfelder, and Broida. 49-65.

Knee, Adam. "The Metamorphosis of the Fly." *Wide Angle* 14.1 (Jan. 1992): 20-34.

Knight, Arthur. "Science-Fiction Friction." *Saturday Review* 5 June 1954: 27.

Knight, David. *The Age of Science: The Scientific World-View in the Nineteenth Century.* Oxford: Blackwell, 1986.

"Known Nuclear Tests Worldwide, 1945-1994." The Bulletin of the Atomic Scientists. Online. Available: <http://www.bullatomsci.org/issues/nukenotes/mj95 nukenote.html>

Krafft-Ebing, R. V. *Psychopathia Sexualis*. Trans. F. J. Rebman. 1906. New York: Physicians and Surgeons, 1922.

Krutnik, Frank. *In a Lonely Street: Film Noir, Genre, Masculinity*. New York: Routledge, 1991.

Lacan, Jacques. *The Four Fundamental Concepts of Psychoanalysis*. Trans. Alan Sheridan. Ed. Jacques Alain Miller. New York: Norton, 1978.

——. "On a Question Preliminary to Any Possible Treatment of Psychosis." *Écrits*. Trans. Alan Sheridan. New York: Norton, 1977. 179-225.

Langmuir, Irving. "An Atomic Arms Race and Its Alternatives." *One World or None*. Eds. Masters and Way. 47-52.

Laplanche, J., and J. B. Pontalis. *The Language of Psychoanalysis*. Trans. Donald Nicholson-Smith. New York: Norton, 1973.

Latham, Rob. "Subterranean Suburbia: Underneath the Small Town Myth in the Two Versions of Invaders from Mars." *Science-Fiction Studies* 22.2 (July 1995): 198-208.

Laura, Ernesto G. "Invasion of the Body Snatchers." *Focus on the Science Fiction Film*. 1957. Ed. William Johnson. Englewood Cliffs, NJ: Prentice-Hall, 1972. 71-73.

Laurence, William. L. *Dawn Over Zero: The Story of the Atomic Bomb*. 1946. 2nd ed. New York: Knopf, 1953.

Leaming, Barbara. *If This Was Happiness: A Biography of Rita Hayworth*. New York: Viking, 1989.

Lem, Stanislaw. "Robots in Science Fiction." *SF: The Other Side of Realism: Essays on Modern Fantasy and Science Fiction*. Ed. Thomas D. Clareson. Trans. Franz Rottensteiner. Bowling Green, OH: Bowling Green State University Popular Press, 1971. 307-25.

Lenihan, John H. "Superweapons from the Past." *Beyond the Stars III: The Material World in American Popular Film*. Eds. Paul Loukides and Linda K. Fuller. Bowling Green, OH: Bowling Green State University Popular Press, 1993. 164-73.

Levenstein, Aaron. *The Atomic Age: Suicide . . . Slavery or Social Planning?* New York: League for Industrial Democracy, 1946.

Levine, Howard, Daniel Jacobs, and Lowell J. Rubin, eds. *Psychoanalysis and the Nuclear Threat*. Hillsdale, NJ: Analytic P, 1988.

Levine, Howard B., and Bennett Simon. Introduction. *Psychoanalysis and the Nuclear Threat*. Eds. Levine, Jacobs, and Rubin. 1-13.

Lifton, Robert Jay, and Greg Mitchell. *Hiroshima in America: Fifty Years of Denial*. New York: Putnam, 1995.

Lindner, Robert. *The Fifty-Minute Hour*. New York: Bantam, 1954.

Lukacs, Georg. *The Historical Novel*. Trans. Hannah and Stanley Mitchell. New York: Humanities P, 1965.

Manley, John H. "A New Laboratory Is Born." *Reminiscences of Los Alamos*.

Eds. Badash, Hirschfelder, and Broida. 21-40.

Masters, Dexter, and Katherine Way, eds. *One World or None*. New York: McGraw-Hill, 1946.

Matheson, Richard. *The Shrinking Man*. 1956. New York: Bantam, 1969.

May, Elaine Tyler. "Explosive Issues: Sex, Women, and the Bomb." *Recasting America: Culture and Politics in the Age of the Cold War.* Ed. Lary May. Chicago: U of Chicago P, 1989. 154-70.

McConnell, Frank D. "Song of Innocence: The Creature from the Black Lagoon." *Journal of Popular Film* 2 (1973): 15-28.

McMillan, Elsie. "Outside the Inner Fence." *Reminiscences of Los Alamos*. Eds. Badash, Hirshfelder, and Broida. 41-47.

Meares, Russell. "The Secret, Lies and the Paranoid Process." *Contemporary Psychoanalysis* 24 (1988): 650-66.

Mechling, Elizabeth Walker, and Jay Mechling. "The Campaign for Civil Defense and the Struggle to Naturalize the Bomb." *Critical Questions: Invention, Creativity, and the Criticism of Discourse and Media*. Eds. William L. Nothstine, Carole Blair, and Gary A. Copeland. New York: St. Martin's, 1994. 125-54.

Meeropol, Robert. "Rosenberg Realities." *Secret Agents*. Eds. Garber and Walkowitz. 235-51.

Metz, Christian. "'Identification, Mirror' and 'The Passion for Perceiving.'" *Defining Cinema*. Ed. Peter Lehman. New Brunswick, NJ: Rutgers UP, 1997. 171-87.

Miller, Douglas T., and Marion Nowak. *The Fifties: The Way We Really Were*. Garden City, NY: Doubleday, 1977.

"Minutes of the Second Meeting of the Target Committee, Los Alamos, May 10-11, 1945." U.S. National Archives, Record Group 77, Records of the Office of the Chief of Engineers, Manhattan Engineering District, TS Manhattan Project File '42-'46, folder 5D Selection of Targets, 2 Notes on Target Committee Meetings.

Mirowsky, John, and Catherine E. Ross. "Paranoia and the Structure of Power-lessness." *American Sociological Review* 48 (1983): 228-39.

The Monolith Monsters. Dir. John Sherwood. Universal, 1957.

Morrison, Philip. "If the Bomb Gets Out of Hand." *One World or None*. Eds. Masters and Way. 1-6.

Mumford, Edwin. *Diary of a Paranoiac: Being a Series of Fictional Associations on the Subject of Fear.* New York: Exposition P, 1964.

Mumford, Lewis. "Gentlemen: You Are Mad!" *Saturday Review of Literature* 2 Mar. 1946: 5-6.

——. *In the Name of Sanity*. New York: Harcourt, Brace, 1954.

Nelson, Joyce. "TV, the Bomb, and the Body." *Secret Agents*. Eds. Garber and Walkowitz. 31-45.

156 · Works Cited

"The New Pictures: *The Day the Earth Stood Still.*" *Time* Oct. 1951: 99-100.

Newhill, Christina E. "The Role of Culture in the Development of Paranoid Symptomatology." *American Journal of Orthopsychiatry* 60 (1990): 176-85.

Niederland, William G. *The Schreber Case: Psychoanalytic Profile of a Paranoid Personality.* New York: Quadrangle, 1974.

O'Donnell, Patrick. "Engendering Paranoia in Contemporary Narrative." *Boundary 2* 19.1 (Spring 1992): 181-204.

Oldham, Stanley, and Stanley Bone, eds. *Paranoia: New Psychoanalytic Perspectives.* Madison, CT: International UP, 1994.

Oppenheimer, J. R. "Atomic Weapons." *Proceedings of the American Philosophical Society* 90 (1946): 7-10.

——. "The New Weapon: The Turn of the Screw." *One World or None.* Eds. Masters and Way. 22-25.

Overstreet, Harry, and Bonaro Overstreet. *What We Must Know About Communism.* New York: Norton, 1958.

"Politics." *Time* 20 Aug. 1945: 29.

Porush, David. *The Soft Machine: Cybernetic Fiction.* New York: Methuen, 1985.

"President Truman Did Not Understand." *U.S. News and World Report* 15 Aug. 1960: 68-71.

Prigogine, Ilya, and Isabelle Stengers. *Order Out of Chaos: Man's New Dialogue with Nature.* New York: Bantam, 1984.

Public Papers of the Presidents of the United States: Harry S. Truman, Containing the Public Messages, Speeches and Statements of the President April 12 to December 31, 1945. Washington, D.C.: GPO, 1945.

Rabinowitch, Eugene. "Five Years After." *Bulletin of the Atomic Scientists* (1951): 3-5, 12.

Revenge of the Creature. Dir. Jack Arnold. Universal, 1955.

Riesman, David. *The Lonely Crowd: A Study of the Changing American Character.* New Haven: Yale UP, 1950.

Robbins, Bruce. "Helpless and Heartless: Irving Howe, James Bond, and the Rosenbergs." *Secret Agents.* Eds. Garber and Walkowitz. 142-54.

Roberts, Robin. *A New Species: Gender and Science in Science Fiction.* Urbana: U of Illinois P, 1993.

Roensch, Eleanor Stone. *Life within Limits.* Los Alamos, NM: Los Alamos Historical Society, 1993.

Rogin, Michael. "Kiss Me Deadly: Communism, Motherhood, and Cold War Movies." *Representations* 6 (Spring 1984): 1-36.

Said, Edward. *Orientalism.* New York: Pantheon, 1978.

Samuels, Stuart. "The Age of Conspiracy and Conformity: *Invasion of the Body Snatchers.*" *American History/American Film: Interpreting the Hollywood*

Image. Eds. John E. O'Connor and Martin A. Jackson. New York: Ungar, 1979. 203-16.

Santner, Eric L. *My Own Private Germany: Daniel Paul Schreber's Secret History of Modernity.* Princeton: Princeton UP, 1996.

Sayre, Nora. *Running Time: Films of the Cold War.* New York: Dial P, 1982.

Schreber, Daniel Paul. *Memoirs of My Nervous Illness.* 1903. Trans. and eds. Ida MacAlpine and Richard A. Hunter. London: Dawson, 1955.

Schrecker, Ellen. *The Age of McCarthyism: A Brief History with Documents.* Boston: Bedford, 1994.

——. "Before the Rosenbergs: Espionage Scenarios in the Early Cold War." *Secret Agents.* Eds. Garber and Walkowitz. 127-41.

"The Screen: Them Are Ants." *Commonweal* 18 June 1954: 269-17.

Segal, Hanna M. "Paranoid Anxiety and Paranoia." *Paranoia.* Eds. Oldham and Bone. 17-26.

——. "Silence Is the Real Crime." *Psychoanalysis and the Nuclear Threat.* Eds. Levine, Jacobs, and Rubin. 35-58.

Shaheen, Jack G., and Richard Taylor. "The Beginning or the End." *Nuclear War Films.* Ed. Jack G. Shaheen. Carbondale: Southern Illinois UP, 1978. 3-10.

Shapiro, Benjamin. "Universal Truths: Cultural Myths and Generic Adaptations in 1950s Science Fiction Films." *Journal of Popular Film and Television* 18.3 (1990): 103-11.

Shapiro, Maurice M. "Observations of the Trinity Test." U.S. National Archives. Record Group 227. OSRD-S1 Committee. Box 82 Folder 6, "Trinity."

Shapley, Harlow. "It's an Old Story with the Stars." *One World or None.* Eds. Masters and Way. 7-10.

Siegel, Ronald. *Whispers: The Voices of Paranoia.* New York: Crown, 1994.

Siegel, Sandra. "Literature and Degeneration: The Representation of 'Decadence.'" *Degeneration.* Eds. Chamberlin and Gilman. 199-219.

Silver, Alain, and Elizabeth Ward, eds. *Film Noir: An Encyclopedic Reference to the American Style.* Woodstock, NY: Overlook P, 1979.

Silverman, Kaja. *Male Subjectivity at the Margins.* New York: Routledge, 1992.

Sobchack, Vivian. *Screening Space: The American Science Fiction Film.* 1980. 2nd ed. New York: Ungar, 1987.

——. "The Virginity of Astronauts: Sex and the Science Fiction Film." *Alien Zone: Cultural Theory and Contemporary Science Fiction Cinema.* London: Verso, 1990. 258-77.

Sontag, Susan. "The Imagination of Disaster." *Against Interpretation.* New York: Anchor, 1966. 201-25.

"Statement by the President of the United States." Trinity Atomic Web Site. Online. Available:< http://www.environlist.org>.

Steinberg, Blema S. "Strategists, Psychoanalysts, and Nuclear Deterrence." *Psy-*

choanalysis and the Nuclear Threat. Eds. Levine, Jacobs, and Rubin. 145-67.

Stimson, Henry L. "The Decision to Use the Atomic Bomb." *Harper's* Feb. 1947: 97-107.

Stone, Albert E. *Literary Aftershocks: American Writers, Readers, and the Bomb*. New York: Twayne, 1994.

Stone, I. F. *The Haunted Fifties*. Boston: Little, Brown, 1963.

Stouffer, Samuel A. *Communism, Conformity, and Civil Liberties: A Cross-Section of the Nation Speaks Its Mind*. New York: Garden City, 1955.

Subversive Influence in the Educational Process. Hearings Before the Subcommittee to Investigate the Administration of the Internal Security Act and Other Internal Security Laws of the Committee on the Judiciary, US Senate, 82nd Congress, 2nd Session, Sept. 8, 9, 10, 23, 25, and Oct. 13, 1952. U.S. Govt. Printing Office, 1952.

Szaz, Ferenc Morton. *The Day the Sun Rose Twice*. Albuquerque: U of New Mexico P, 1984.

Tarratt, Margaret. "Monsters from the Id." *Film Genre Reader*. Ed. Barry Keith Grant. Austin: U of Texas P, 1986. 104-14.

Tausk, Victor. "On the Origin of the 'Influencing Machine' in Schizophrenia." *Psychoanalytic Quarterly* 2 (1933): 519-56.

Taylor, Bryan C. "Register of the Repressed: Women's Voice and Body in the Nuclear Weapons Organization." *Quarterly Journal of Speech* 79 (1993): 267-85.

——. *"Reminiscences of Los Alamos:* Narrative, Critical Theory, and the Organizational Subject." *Critical Questions: Invention, Creativity, and the Criticism of Discourse and Media*. Eds. William L. Nothstine, Carole Blair, and Gary A. Copeland. New York: St. Martin's, 1994. 423-47.

Taylor, Richard. "Hiroshima: A Document of the Atomic Bombing." *Nuclear War Films*. Ed. Jack G. Shaheen. Carbondale: Southern Illinois UP, 1978. 127-31.

Taylor, Walter G. "Letter." *Time* 27 Aug. 1945. 2.

Them! Dir. Gordon Douglas. Warner, 1954.

"Them!" Catholic World May 1954: 144.

"The 36-Hour War." *Life* 19 Nov. 1945: 27-35.

This Island Earth. Dir. Joseph Newman. Universal, 1954.

Titus, A. Constandina, and Jerry L. Simich. "From 'Atomic Bomb Baby' to 'Nuclear Funeral': Atomic Music Comes of Age, 1945-1990." *Popular Music and Society* 14.4 (Winter 1990): 11-37.

Torry, Robert. "Apocalypse Then: Benefits of the Bomb in Fifties Science Fiction Films." *Cinema Journal* 31.1 (Fall 1991): 7-21.

Truman, Harry S. Memoirs: *Volume One: Year of Decisions*. Garden City, NY: Doubleday, 1955.

Tudor, Andrew. *Monsters and Mad Scientists: A Cultural History of the Horror Movie*. London: Blackwell, 1989.

20 Million Miles to Earth. Dir. Nathan Juran. Columbia, 1957.

Urey, Harold C. "How Does It All Add Up?" *One World or None*. 53-58.

"U.S. and the World." *Time* 20 Aug. 1945: 29.

Vattimo, Gianni. "The End of (Hi)story." *Zeitgeist in Babel*. Ed. Ingelborg Hoestery. Bloomington: Indiana UP, 1991.

Vonnegut, Kurt. *Cat's Cradle*. 1963. New York: Bantam, 1988.

Walsh, Moira. "Films." *America* 3 July 1954: 367.

Wangh, Martin. "On Aggression: The Psychological Fallout of Surface Nuclear Testing." *American Imago* 38.3 (Fall 1981): 305-22.

The War of the Worlds. Dir. Byron Haskin. Paramount, 1953.

Warren, Bill. *Keep Watching the Skies!: American Science Fiction Movies of the Fifties. Vol. I. 1950-1957*. London: McFarland, 1982.

Warren, Col. Stafford. "Trinity Test, July 16, 1945—Radiation Monitoring." U.S. National Archives, Record Group 77, Records of the Office of the Chief of Engineers, Manhattan Engineering District, TS Manhattan Project Files, Folder 4, "Trinity Test."

Weart, Spencer. *Nuclear Fear: A History of Images*. Cambridge: Harvard UP, 1988.

Weiss, Allen S. "The Other as Muse: On the Ontology and Aesthetics of Narcissism." *Psychosis*. Eds. Allison, et al. 70-87.

Wells, H. G. "The Empire of the Ants." *H. G. Wells: Short Stories*. Ed. Tim Heald. London: Folio Society, 1990. 1-16.

——. *The War of the Worlds*. 1898. New York: Bantam, 1988.

Wells, Paul. "The Invisible Man: Shrinking Masculinity in the 1950s Science Fiction B-Movie." *You Tarzan: Masculinity, Movies and Men*. Eds. Pat Kirkham and Janet Thurman. New York: St. Martin's, 1993. 181-99.

"When Atom Bomb Struck—Uncensored." *Life* 29 Sept. 1952: 19-26.

White, Robert B. "The Mother-Conflict in Schreber's Psychosis." *The International Journal of Psychoanalysis* 42 (1961): 55-73.

Wittner, Lawrence. *Cold War America: From Hiroshima to Watergate*. New York: Praeger, 1974.

"A World Worth Waiting For." *Coronet* 1 Nov. 1948: 31-38.

Wylie, Philip. "Science Fiction and Sanity in an Age of Crisis." *Modern Science Fiction: Its Meaning and Its Future*. Ed. Reginald Bretnor. New York: Coward-McCann, 1953.

Yavenditti, Michael J. "John Hersey and the American Conscience: The Reception of 'Hiroshima.'" *Pacific Historical Review* 43.1 (Feb. 1974): 24-49.

INDEX

Adams, Henry 11

Alperovitz, Gar 16, 24, 25, 120, 132-33

Amazing Colossal Man, The 63

Attack of the 50 Ft. Woman 4, 51, 60-63

Badash, Lawrence 17

Bartter, Martha A. 104

Bataille, Georges 102, 132, 142

Bates, Harry 31, 133

Beast from 20,000 Fathoms, The 4, 75, 77-79, 141

Beginning or the End, The 42, 131-32, 144

Bethe, Hans 25

Bikini Atoll 15, 41, 44, 125

Biskind, Peter 31, 129, 135, 138

Blade Runner 13

Bohr, Niels 27-28

Boyer, Paul 15, 18, 29, 42, 94, 118, 129, 131, 137, 138, 140, 144

Bradbury, Ray 14, 138

Bradley, David, *No Place to Hide* 3, 15-16, 41, 42, 43, 49

Brode, Bernice 52

Brode, Robert 52

Brown, Harrison 76, 77

Cameron, Norman 28-29, 54, 58, 60

Capek, Karl, *R.U.R.* 13

Caruth, Cathy 101-02, 132

Civil Defense 7, 78, 97-98, 118-19

Compton, Arthur 27, 117

Compton, Karl T. 114

Creature from the Black Lagoon, The 4, 91, 92-97

Creature Walks Among Us, The 141

Darwin, Charles 10, 11, 75, 81, 84, 88

Day the Earth Stood Still, The 3, 23, 26, 27, 28-29, 30-31, 133

Deadly Mantis, The 141

Derrida, Jacques 2

De Seversky, Major Alexander P. 117, 144

Earth vs. the Flying Saucers 4, 101, 105-07

Ehrenreich, Barbara 94, 140

Einstein, Albert 17, 25, 28, 31

Ellegard, Alvar 10

Ellis, Albert, *American Sexual Tragedy, The* 95, 96-97

Enola Gay 15

Enriquez, Michelle 9, 20, 131

Ferenczi, Sandor 92

Fermi, Enrico 51-52, 80

Fermi, Laura 51-52, 80

Feynman, Richard P. 15, 18-19

Film noir 3, 130

Finney, Jack 44, 47, 135

Frankenstein 23, 24, 38

Franklin, H. Bruce 104

Freud, Sigmund 2, 3, 7, 11, 12, 19-20, 34-35, 39-40, 54-56, 58, 61-62, 92, 130, 131, 132, 136, 142

Fuchs, Klaus 32